fast & easy
SCRAPBOOKING

MEMORY
MAKERS
BOOKS

contents

fast & easy scrapbooking

72

44

6

Executive Editor Deborah Mock
Art Director Mark Lewis
Associate Editor Darlene D'Agostino
Craft Editor Kari Hansen-Daffin
Departments Editor Trisha McCarty-Luedke
Editorial Assistant Sarah Kelly
Senior Graphic Designer Dawn Knutson
Photographer Ken Trujillo
Idea Editor Shawna Rendon
Idea Coordinator Lynda Meisner
Editorial Support Dena Twinem

F+W Publications, Inc.
Chairman William F. Reilly
President Stephen J. Kent
Executive Vice President & CFO Mark F. Arnett

F+W Publications, Inc. Magazine Division
President William R. Reed
Vice President Consumer Marketing Susan Dubois
Director of Business Planning & Analysis Matt Friedersdorf
Publication Production Manager Vicki Whitford

Contributors
Contributing Writer Brandi Ginn

Contributing Artists Leah Blanco Williams, Joanna Bolick, Amy Goldstein, Michelle Pesce,
Heather Preckel, Elizabeth Ruuska, Becky Thompson, Suzy West

Contributing Designers Sarah Daniels, Jeff Norgord, Karen Roehl, Melanie Warner

Contributing Photographer Lizzy Creazzo, Jennifer Reeves

2005 Memory Makers Masters Jessie Baldwin, Jenn Brookover, Christine Brown, Sheila Doherty,
Jodi Heinen, Jeniece Higgins, Nic Howard, Julie Johnson,
Shannon Taylor, Samantha Walker

Special Thanks
We would like to thank all contributors to this book, including those participants whose pages we requested but were not able to feature because of space limitations. We appreciate your willingness to share your ideas—you are what makes this magazine unique.

The material in this book appeared in the previously published Volume 10, No. 8 issue of *Memory Makers*, a division of F+W Publications, Inc., and appears here by permission of the contributors.

Published by Memory Makers Books, an imprint of F+W Publications, Inc.
12365 Huron Street, Suite 500, Denver, CO 80234
Phone 1-800-254-9124

First edition. Printed in the United States of America.

09 08 07 06 05 5 4 3 2 1

A catalog record for this book is available from the Library of Congress
at <http://catalog.loc.gov>.

ISBN 1-892127-71-7

Distributed in Canada by Fraser Direct
100 Armstrong Avenue
Georgetown, ON, Canada L7G 5S4
Tel: (905) 877-4411

Distributed in the U.K. and Europe by David & Charles
Brunel House, Newton Abbot, Devon,
TQ12 4PU, England
Tel: (+44) 1626 323200, Fax: (+44) 1626 323319
Email: mail@davidandcharles.co.uk

Distributed in Australia by Capricorn Link
P.O. Box 704, S. Windsor, NSW 2756 Australia
Tel: (02) 4577-3555

Memory Makers Books is the home of *Memory Makers*, the scrapbook magazine dedicated to educating and inspiring scrapbookers. *Memory Makers* features the ideas and stories of our readers around the world—people who believe in keeping scrapbooks and the tradition of the family photo historian alive. *Memory Makers* is committed to providing ideas and inspiration for this worldwide community of scrapbookers. To subscribe, or for more information, call 1-800-366-6465.

Visit us on the Internet at www.memorymakersmagazine.com.

fw
F+W PUBLICATIONS, INC.

book index

an index of scrapbook page ideas, products and techniques featured in this book

Simplify It, p. 64

Color Wheel Recipes, p. 36

featured scrapbookers

Meet the scrapbookers whose ideas are featured in this book. Each of these contributors receives a gift box containing scrapbook supplies generously donated by leading scrapbook-product manufacturers.

Alabama
Beverly Sizemore – Sulligent

Alaska
Stephanie Rarick
– Anchorage

Arizona
Melissa Koehler – Surprise

Arkansas
Delaney Butler – Fayetteville

California
Miki Benedict – Modesto
Elsie Bustamante
– Chula Vista
Diana Hudson – Bakersfield
Pamela James – Ventura
Johanna Peterson
– El Cajon
Kimberley Wood
– Thousand Oaks

Colorado
Kelly Angard
– Highlands Ranch
Kelli Noto – Centennial
Brandi Ginn – Longmont

Georgia
Danielle Thompson – Tucker

Idaho
M Sheila Doherty – Coeur d'Alene

Illinois
M Jeniece Higgins – Lake Forest
Courtney Walsh – Winnebago

Indiana
Lisa Dorsey – Westfield
Katy Jurasevich – Valparaiso

Kentucky
Erin Wells – Elsmere

Maryland
Tracy Miller – Fallston

Massachusetts
Alison Chabe – Charlestown

Michigan
Jennifer Bourgeault
– Macomb Township

Minnesota
Linda Albrecht – St. Peter
M Christine Brown – Hanover
Sherrill Ghilardi Pierre
– Maplewood
Vicki Harvey – Champlin
M Jodi Heinen – Sartell
Sue Thomas – Anoka
Susan Weinroth – Centerville

Mississippi
Angelia Wigginton – Belmont

Missouri
Melanie Bauer – Columbia

Nevada
M Jessie Baldwin – Las Vegas

Ohio
Kimberly Brock – Maineville
Stephanie Carpenter
– Sandusky
Amanda Goodwin
– Munroe Falls

Oklahoma
Susan Cyrus – Broken Arrow

Oregon
Kim Mauch – Portland

Pennsylvania
Marla Kress – Cheswick

Rhode Island
Catherine Mathews-Scanlon
– Middletown

Tennessee
Brandi Barnes – Kelso
Alison Lockett – Knoxville
M Shannon Taylor – Bristol

Texas
M Jenn Brookover – San Antonio
Sandra Hicks – San Antonio
Kristin Holly – Katy
M Julie Johnson – Seabrook
Pam Sivage – Georgetown
Wendy Tuten – Terrell

Utah
Michelle Coleman – Layton
Kara Henry – Provo

Virginia
Kelli Lawlor – Norfolk

International

Canada
Tania Duczak
– Montreal, Quebec
Cari Locken
– Edmonton, Alberta
Heather Main
– Langley, British Columbia
Valerie Maltais
– Sherbrooke, Quebec
Shelley Rankin
– Fredericton, New Brunswick
Gislaine Vincent
– Dorval, Quebec

England
Caroline Howe
– Hornchurch, Essex

New Zealand
M Nic Howard
– Pukekohe, South Auckland

M This logo denotes a current *Memory Makers* Master.

Make It Your Own, p. 10

Color Wheel Recipes, p. 36

make it your own

Turning pre-fab page kits into ab-fab layouts

by Kelly Angard

Page kits offer solutions to several problems of the time-strapped scrapbooker—the supplies are pre-coordinated to make shopping a snap, their streamlined style and design are great for theme albums, and they can increase productivity by contributing to speedy layout construction. But, does opting for pre-coordinated page kits to save time have to mean sacrificing style? No—just think of a page kit as a colored canvas waiting for an absolutely fabulous personal touch. On the following pages, several quick-and-easy techniques are combined with page kits to prove that pre-fab does not mean cookie-cutter. Look at these speedy techniques to see how they can be adapted to any page kit on the market, no matter its design, theme or color.

easy glitz

The stylized designs and textured paper in this kit evoke a bit of whimsy that is fresh and contemporary. Danielle Thompson of Tucker, Georgia, demonstrates how a little gold and glitter can go a long way without overpowering her photos and patterned papers. Subtle detailing is achieved with a gold paint pen. Danielle painted the strawberry seeds on the patterned paper, a photo of a painted sunflower and also filled in some of the white polka-dots on the background paper. Sprinkling glitter onto adhesive dots add a bit of flashy fun when used sparingly over penned swirls and stripes.

supplies: Page kit (Waste Not Paper) • Gold paint pen (Krylon) • Gel pen (Marvy) • Glitter paint (Ranger) • Zots adhesive dots (Therm O Web)

Waste Not Paper
Strawberry Kit
• 2 sheets solid 12 x 12" paper
• assorted decorative/textured paper blocks
• 4 shaped cards and envelopes

thoughtful

Here you are, so pure & innocent watching airplanes in the sky. I wonder what you are thinking in your 17 month mind. When will you start remembering things? Chances are, you won't remember this day. But we both can remember b/c of this page. At this time in your life you loved airplanes.

easy stamping

Jeniece Higgins (Masters '05) enhanced the texture of this kit's linenlike cardstock with easy stamping techniques. The large letter stamps inked with acrylic paint transform the large tag into a layered title. Three flower motif stamps—a large and small daisy and a fine-detail shadow stamp also inked with acrylic paint—delicately balance the design. If selecting stamps to match a layout seems to make your head spin, purchase a set of tried-and-true geometric shapes or a basic pattern stamp with a stripe design that you can grab when you're short on time.

supplies: Page kit (Chatterbox) • Stamps (EK Success, Hero Arts, Making Memories, Stampin' Up) • Stamping ink (Stazon by Tsukineko, Stampin' Up) • Acrylic paint (Plaid) • Pearls

variations

- Add a fun look to a die cut or tag with the addition of a polka-dot stamp.
- Make a statement with a collage of letter stamps in a variety of sizes and font styles.
- Stamp a bold design over a striped patterned paper for a cool, graphic effect.
- Add texture and elegance to any stamped image by heating a sprinkle of embossing powder for a shiny finish.

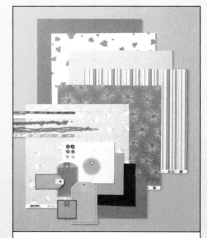

Chatterbox
Reading Room Kit

- 6 sheets 12 x 12" patterned papers
- 5 stitched tags
- 20 strands ribbon/fiber
- 12 rivets paper fasteners
- 12 photo mats
- layout ideas

Sanook Paper Company

Holiday Scrapper's Pack Theme Kit

- handmade paper:
  - 4 sheets 12 x 12" solid
  - 4 1½ x 12" torn strips
  - 6 sheets 5 x 7" solid
- 30 die cuts
- 8 skeleton leaves
- 11 paper leaves and flowers
- 8 bowed ribbons
- 3 strands paper string
- 2 strips woven mesh
- layout ideas

easy inking

Julie Johnson (Masters '05) added quick color and dimension to cut and torn papers and to die-cut shapes by swiping the edges with an ink pad. She dramatically enhanced the texture of handmade paper by rubbing an ink pad over the top of the paper's crumpled peaks. Dark colored or patterned papers will glow with swipes of white ink or become grungy and graphic with a few rough swipes of black ink. Dab specific areas of a die cut or journaling block with a cosmetic sponge loaded with ink. Blend as desired.

supplies: Page kit (Sanook) • Rub-ons (Making Memories) • Colorbox Fluid Chalk brown stamping ink (Clearsnap) • Sandpaper • Computer font

Christmas time is my favorite time of year. Things are really busy for us. Every year we have a party for our friends and their children, complete with Santa. All the kids bring a gift, and Santa passes them out, not without a picture of course! You're still a little scared of Santa, so I settled on pictures in front of the tree instead.

Dec 2004

CHRISTMAS

variations

- Squeeze re-inker colors onto wax paper, roll over with a brayer and then onto cardstock for a quick, even coat of color.
- Drip re-inker into a bowl, add water and brush on a colorful ink wash.
- Adhere vertical or horizontal strips of artist's tape onto cardstock; press ink pads over taped cardstock. Carefully peel tape off to reveal perfectly straight lines.

easy machine-stitching

This kit features elements with the look of stitching, so a little machine-stitching goes a long way to enhance this layout. Diana Hudson (Masters '03) created machine-stitched stems to add a touch of tailored simplicity to flowers punched from the kit's sherbert-colored patterned papers. Stitched details also are a great way to add clean lines of color and texture to a layout. You may need to adjust the tension on your sewing machine and increase stitch length for a smooth stitching line.

supplies: Page kit (Fancy Pants) • Flower punch (EK Success) • Tags (Making Memories) • Brads

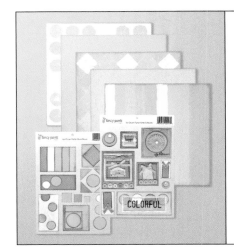

Fancy Pants Designs

Ice Cream Parlor Kit

- 8 sheets 12 x 12" patterned paper
- 4 sheets solid paper
- 2 sheets cardstock accent stickers

[Just because]

Affectionate definitely describes you! I love that you never need a reason to kiss me —you just always seem to know when I need one! Keep the kisses coming, kissy girl!

a kiss and a hug just because

variations

- Bring attention to a matted photo or title block by stitching a border in a contrasting color.
- Intersperse stitching between strips of patterned paper.
- Border your layout with a large zigzag stitch for a bit of whimsical fun.

variations

- Use a simple chain-stitch over a swatch of fabric for a sweet shabby-chic title.
- Integrate beads or sequins with stitches for a bit of sparkle and shine.
- Stitch several patterned paper tiles together to form a pleasing horizontal or vertical border.

easy hand-stitching

Pamela James of Ventura, California, adds a touch of handcrafted charm with stitched details to this page kit, which is steeped in traditional style and rustic colors. Pamela secured the kit's die-cut embellishments with simple cross-stitches and paired straight stitches with copper brads as a photo-corner accent. To ensure precise needle placement, pre-pierce holes with a thin needle or paper piercer. Trade embroidery floss for colorful, textured fibers and watch how a little bit of stitching can make a big statement.

supplies: Page kit (Déjà Views by C-Thru Ruler) • Embroidery floss (DMC) • Stamping inks (Clearsnap) • Brads (Jo-Ann)

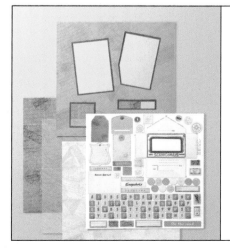

Déjà Views Windows

Exploration Kit by C-Thru Ruler

- 4 sheets 12 x 12" patterned papers with frame windows
- 4 coordinating mats
- patterned vellum and parchment
- sheet of die cuts
- layout ideas

The handwritten journaling on the photo reads: Olivia, this photo of you makes me remember just how much I loved kittens when I was your age. My two sisters didn't seem nearly as enthralled with them as I was. You will sit and giggle at her antics, or follow her around the yard as she plays. I thought it would be hard for you to choose only one kitten from Prissy's litter of five, but you handled it quite well. Summer, 2004

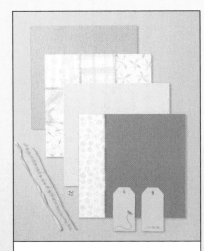

Memory Stitches
Pastel Quilt Kit
- 2 sheets 12 x 12" embroidered, patterned paper
- 2 sheets 12 x 12" solid paper
- 2 embroidered tags
- fibers
- eyelets
- layout ideas

easy ribbon

Angelia Wigginton of Belmont, Mississippi, used simple, knotted gingham ribbon on rickrack borders to complement this kit's pre-stitched paper. As a decorative element, ribbons add texture and color without adding weight or bulk to your page. And there's nothing quicker than tying ribbon to a tag, charm or punched shape. Or, try stitching a wide ribbon on three sides to make a pocket for tags or extra photos.

supplies: Page kit (Memory Stitches) • Rickrack • Ribbon (Close to My Heart) • Letter stickers (Heidi Grace) • Photo corners • Buttons

variations
- Staple ribbons to your page for fast frills.
- Layer sheer ribbon over a photo or stamped design for transparent color.
- Weave patterned ribbons together for a striking and colorful accent.
- Lace velvet ribbon through attached eyelets to resemble a corset for a feminine look.

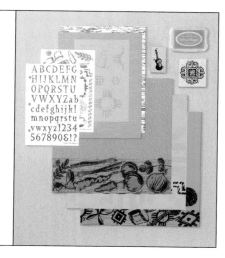

Club Scrap
Salsa Kit

- 10 sheets each
  8½ x 11" and 12 x 12"
  exclusive patterned
  paper, embossed
  solid paper
- 4 sheets die-cut tags
- 2 sheets embossed,
  themed images
- stencil sheet
- 2 rubber stamps, ink pad
- 4 ball chains
- layout ideas

easy painting

Kelly Angard of Highlands Ranch, Colorado, softened her kit's bright papers with a light wash of color using acrylic paint and baby wipes. Squeeze a dollop of paint onto a paper plate. Scrunch a baby wipe in your fingers; press into paint and then onto the paper a few times leaving a good amount of paint on the page. Quickly grab a new baby wipe, flatten out and wipe across page to blend paint spots together. The more you rub, the more paint will be removed, giving you a soft wash with a hint of color. Try blending two or three colors together in the same fashion to create a gradient effect.

supplies: Page kit (Club Scrap) • Acrylic paint • Hole, circle punches • Letter stickers (American Crafts, KI Memories, SEI) • Rub-on letters (Li'l Davis) • Black pen • Corner rounder

variations

- Use paint with foam stamps for grunge or shabby-chic elegance.
- Flick a toothbrush loaded with paint across your page for spotted texture.
- Use a soft wash of watercolor to enhance an embossed design.
- Squeeze a dollop of acrylic paint into a spray bottle, add water and shake; spritz over solid or patterned paper for an artistic effect.

New York

My gARDen

DIARY

bind-it-yourself
albums

Smart and simple techniques for making your own album by Debbie Mock

With just a few fun supplies from your craft room and a simple plan to hold them together, you could easily assemble a creative album with a personal touch. Sandi Genovese, creative director at Mrs. Grossman's Paper Company and host of the television show "DIY Scrapbooking," loves to make small theme albums celebrating topics such as her siblings, Christmases and trips. Because of Sandi's artistic nature, she also appreciates the freedom to decorate her own covers, which traditional bindings do not easily allow. So she began experimenting.

"I found that there are lots of inexpensive, durable items used to hold things together, such as metal rings, ball chains, metal prong fasteners and even feed tags," Sandi says. "They are easy to find, easy to customize, and because you are not spending money on an album, you have money left in your budget to play with other things, such as embellishments."

These binding techniques allow for total control, Sandi says. "Everything is open. You can make the albums whatever color or size and as simple or extravagant as you like. There is no limit to the sophistication you can give them."

Be inspired to construct beautiful scrapbooks in a snap by the following creatively-bound albums.

metal binder-ring album

Amy Goldstein of Kent Lakes, New York, bound her bright New York Garden Diary by punching holes in each page and the cover in which to snap colored metal binder rings. To save the time sometimes needed to coordinate papers, Amy used a selection of matching papers that came packaged together with other embellishments. In place of actual stitching, Amy stamped light blue stitches. Fabric strips tied to the metal binder rings add a decorative, finishing touch.

supplies: Déjà Views Fresh Print Collection patterned papers, Wonderful Words rub-ons (C-Thru) • Alphabet buttons, twill, binder rings (Junkitz) • Ribbon (Offray) • Gin-X fabric (Imagination Project) • Chipboard letters (Heidi Swapp) • Spiral feed tags (Kuhl Corporation) • Fusible adhesive (Stitch Witch)

binding variations

fabric twist ties

Inspired by Sandi's idea, Amy created a soft alternative to the metal-ring binding—fabric twist ties. She tore two strips of fabric, placed a strip of fusible adhesive and a narrow gauge wire between the fabric strips and ironed all pieces together.

spiral feed tags

Sandi discovered that plastic feed-tag rings, such as the ones shown left, bind albums quickly and securely.

For quick journaling, Amy ran her patterned paper through her printer. For the right-hand page above, she adhered a strip of striped paper to the background paper before running it through the printer.

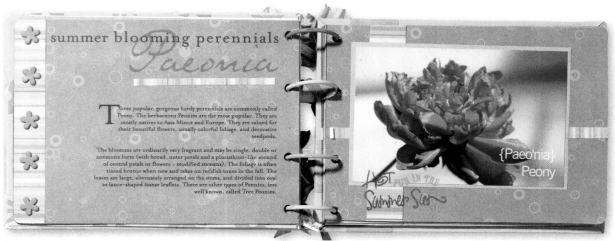

To personalize the look of the album, Amy added complementary flower brads to paper strips on each page. To hide the brad's prongs, she attached the brads before adhering the paper to the page.

To reflect the text printed on the photos, Amy added descriptive rub-ons on the page around each photo.

ball-and-chain album

When Sandi created the original idea for a make-it-yourself album held together with a ball chain, she customized a sleeve to protect it. To create her version of the idea, shown here, Brandi Ginn (Masters '03) cut 5 x 8" rectangles from coordinating cardstock for her background pages. Each page is designed with a picture of her daughter, Natalie, highlighted by a combination of patterned paper and fabric stickers. To soften the look of the metal binding, Brandi added a polka-dot ribbon and heart charm to the ball chain. See right for instructions to make the sleeve.

supplies: Dark, medium and light pink papers (Bazzill) • Patterned papers (KI Memories) • Premade accents (KI Memories) • Acrylic flower, rub-on letters, jewel, chipboard numbers (Heidi Swapp) • Brads (Lasting Impressions, Making Memories) • Fabric stickers (Mrs. Grossman's) • Adhesive dots (Therm O Web) • Black pen • Green pencil • Staples • Ribbon • Paper flowers • Page pebbles

sleeve pattern

To make the sleeve, cut a piece of paper in a shape similar to the one shown below using the height, width and thickness of your completed album to gauge the size. Score on dotted lines, fold in flap a, then b and c, and adhere. With a circle punch, make a notch in the top center for easy album removal.

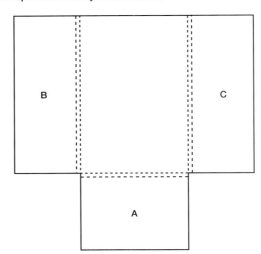

To reinforce the holes through which the ball chain runs, Brandi set an eyelet in the hole on each page.

By placing a frame over a portion of the picture, Brandi drew attention to her daughter's tiny fingers.

Brandi used all black-and white-photos to unify the look of her album.

Brandi simplified the supply selection process by limiting the number of colors used in the album.

accordion-style envelope album

The combination of inexpensive envelopes and a coordinating paper line made this album by Kari Hansen, craft editor, come together quickly (see steps for envelope accordion below). Kari created folio closures to hold the cover closed; Sandi also suggests experimenting with magnet strips or velcro.

supplies: Black, colored papers (Prism) • Black square envelopes • Patterned papers, envelope seals, self-adhesive ribbon, brads (Die Cuts With a View) • Stamps, dye inks (Stampin' Up) • Watercolor paints • Circle punches • Corner rounder • Eyelets • Embroidery floss • Black thread • Dateline font (oldtype.8m.com)

Made just for you with lots of love!

step by step

envelope accordion

1. For accordion pockets: Fold envelope flap backwards. Tuck and adhere flap into the top of another envelope for each pocket. **2.** For the folder: Measure the envelope's height plus the page tabs and cut a paper strip to this height and 2¹/₂ times the envelope's width. **3.** In the middle of the paper strip, score two vertical lines just wider than the envelope's width. Score a parallel line on each side of the first scored lines to accommodate the accordion's depth. Fold on scored lines. Adhere back pocket to the center of the strip. Trim cover overlap.

4. For folio closures: Mat two sets of circle stickers on paper with floss in between one set. Set an eyelet in the center of each folio.

May 2005

Dear Grandma & Grandpa:

I hope you enjoy this little collection of pages, full of people who love you lots and lots. As you look at each page, remember that we love you so much because you first loved us so well. We are very lucky bunch to have you in our lives. Parents to two, grandparents to three, great-grandparents to four (and hopefully more!) and adopted by all spouses, you have definitely earned your G's! You are so dear to us all!

xoxo -
Kari

Connie and Tracy

Kari cut each page slightly smaller than the envelopes to the bulk created by the addition of decorative papers and embellishments. A paper square was decorated and adhered to the front of the first envelope to cover seams.

Round envelope seals act as page tabs and were attached at the top of each page to make them easier to slide in and out of the envelopes.

Sarah

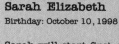

Sarah Elizabeth
Birthday: October 10, 1998

Sarah will start first grade in the upcoming school year. In kindergarten, she learned the whole alphabet and to add and subtract. Sarah has also learned to read and has finished her first book! Sarah loves to dress up and her favorite color is pink. She adores her big brother Steven. She loves to play outside with Steven and looks forward to being big enough to ride motorbikes with the boys. She can now ride a bicycle without training wheels. Sarah loves to pick dandelions and lie in the grass while singing songs about God. She also helps God keep track of the clouds. Sarah has no problem being in front of people and has helped her family lead worship at church. She has learned many Bible verses in Awanas Club this year.

In addition to the coordinating paper line and embellishments, Kari incorporated stitching, tags and a rounded photo corner on each page to unify the design.

The back of each of Kari's pages includes a special journaled message from or about the person pictured on the front.

metal-fastener album

Sheila Doherty (Masters '05) was inspired by Sandi's idea of using metal prong fasteners, usually used for office filing, to bind her Disney album. To simplify the creation of her design, Sheila also used an 8 x 8" Disney paper pack filled with patterned papers, letters and accents. For her cover, she punched a variety of circles to create the whimsical Mickey silhouettes.

supplies: Solid papers, Disney patterned paper (Hot Off The Press) • Prong fasteners • Green gingham ribbon (American Crafts) • Pink gingham ribbon (KI Memories) • Blue and black ribbons • Label maker (Dymo) • Button alphabet stamps (PSX) • Black stamping ink • Ultra Thick Embossing Enamel (Ranger) • Versamark watermark stamping ink (Tsukineko) • Large circle punch (Marvy) • Medium circle punch (McGill) • Small circle punch (Carl) • Circle frame die (Sizzix) • Computer font

metal-prong fastener

The metal prong fastener makes a quick binding for a handmade album. To create the album, cut the pages and covers from cardstock. Score the inside of the pages and covers for easy movement. Adjust the punch width on a three-hole punch to punch only two holes. Punch holes in the pages and the two covers. To bind the album together, slip front cover flap, all pages and back cover flap onto the prongs, place the top piece in place, fold down the prongs and secure them with the sliders.

Rebekah's favorite ride at Disneyland was the Dumbo ride. When she was waiting in line, she was given a magic feather just like in the movie to mark her place in line. Once we got inside Dumbo, she loved that she could make Dumbo go up and down all by herself by just pushing a lever. We went on that ride several times that day to Rebekah's delight.

REBEKAH LOVES DUMBO

Sheila incorporated the metal prongs into the design of the album, decorating them with ribbon to soften the look of the metal. Most border stickers also work well to embellish the fasteners.

Rebekah was just tall enough to ride the rockets in Tomorrowland. While I pushed Luke around in the stroller (who was sad because he was too short to ride), Daddy took Rebekah on the ride.

RIDE

The coordinated paper pack Sheila used included small matching accents, such as the Mickey letters used in the title of each page. To make the letters pop, Sheila coated them with extra thick embossing enamel and adhered them to the page with foam adhesive.

FUN FAMILY

This was Luke's first visit to Disneyland at just 1 1/2 years old. We spent most of our time in Fantasyland with him riding the smaller rides. Disneyland is a magical place even for adults, but for children even more so. Luke was delighted with all the rides, the sights & sounds. Seeing his excitement was the best part of the day.

A simple photo-centric design and coordinating product line made this small album come together quickly.

TimeSavers

17 products to trim the time it takes to create a layout

by Michelle Pesce (Masters '04)

Small children, a busy career, soccer-mom responsibilities...no matter what your path in life, time never seems to slow down when you need it to. More often than not, the craziness of everyday life trumps the already minimal scrapbooking time one has, and tragically, this results in few finished layouts. While this article has no magic formulas for converting your days from 24 hours to 30, the 17 products included will help streamline your creative process, unleash your inspiration and allow you to make the most of the few moments you do find to sit down to scrapbook. From easier measuring to organizing page kits and journaling help to quick and quiet eyelets, the products included will help trim the time it takes to create great layouts.

in-a-dash distressing

My Mind's Eye (**mymindseyeinc.com**) creates mess-free, stress-free distressing with the new Dee's Designs Distressed Effects. These rub-ons emulate the look of dry-brushing, painting, sanding or inking without any of the effort, cleanup time or expense for paints, inks or other tools. Some of the effects are distinct patterns such as flowers to give you the same look as a printed overlay but without the buckling, glare and adhesive issues of using transparencies. Also part of the Dee's Designs line are Unhinged—photorealistic sticker hinges (shown on page above). Pre-scored for easy folding, they lend the stylized look of metal hinges without any of the bulk or complication of attaching real hinges. Distressed Effects $2.99; Unhinged $1.99

step by step

Texturize a layout by simply applying the rub-on with a wooden stick.

a LiTTLe Vintage Flair

factor so together we checked out the sales while I still lived in Kansas City. But when it came down to it, eBay was the right answer for me! I spotted an elegant dusty blue taffeta dress with a black vintage-style lace overlay and a sweet little bow in the middle. It was "bridesmaid" appropriate and still totally me! I ended up winning it for under $40 including shipping!

These are the initial pictures that I emailed to Sarah and the other girls for their thumbs up. (Obviously, I still needed to get the hem taken up.) Fortunately for me, they loved it. And slowly, one by one, the girls each found bridesmaid dresses of their own. All the dresses ended up having a little vintage flavor.

-- Spring 2005

I was *thrilled* when Sarah asked me to be one of the bridesmaids for her and Jonathan's September 24th, 2005 wedding. Of course I would! Sarah is so fun and easy-going that she left it up to us to pick our own bridesmaid dresses. Hello! An excuse to shop for a formal gown and the choice was all mine? Now that's my idea of a good time. Of course cost was a

ART: LEAH BLANCO WILLIAMS

measuring mojo

Perfectly centered titles and elements give a polished look to your pages, and the Déjà Views Zero Hero Centering Ruler from C-Thru Ruler (**dejaviews.com**) makes it possible by easing time-consuming mental gymnastics. Center the clear plastic ruler on top of your page, and the zero marks the spot, exactly dead center. The ruler also includes holes for precisely marking holes for hand-stitching and setting eyelets as well as slots for penciling in quick-and-easy lines for accurately spaced journaling. $3.49 (12"); $4.99 (18")

step by step

Use the Zero Hero ruler for evenly-spaced letter stickers. Gently adhere bottom of stickers to ruler, spacing as desired, and transfer to page.

ribbon rescue

Up until now, one of the biggest challenges in working with ribbon has been adhering it to the page without it making a mess, shifting, bunching, sliding or otherwise wandering away from where you want it to be. Die Cuts With a View (**diecutswithaview.com**) provides an elegant solution to this problem with its self-adhesive ribbon. These $^3/_8$" and $^5/_8$" grosgrain ribbons come in monochromatic packs of three ribbons each (there are 18 different color sets available), and have a strip of adhesive across the back. All you need to do is trim the ribbon to size, peel off the backing and smooth it down. $2.99

ART: HEATHER PRECKEL

page-kits, pronto

Page kits optimize your scrapbooking efficiency by corralling your layout necessities. The Croppin' Companion's (**croppincompanion .com**) innovative page-kit folders help make your kits even more efficient. This sturdy storage system has space for two 12 x 12" or smaller layouts, including a large top-loading pocket and two smaller expandable pockets perfect for photos or embellishments. The pockets are staggered, allowing multiple folders to nest neatly together in any standard size 12 x 12" three-ring binder. The folders are translucent so it's easy to identify which theme or page each folder holds. $9.99 per pack of two folders

ART AND PHOTOS:
MICHELLE PESCE (MASTERS '04)

To be a boy: construction equipment and mountains of dirt, assorted rocks outside and *inside* the house, sandy shores at the bank of the river, trucks that "honk" and "beep", air brakes that "swish," parked tractors silently begging for someone to climb on them, the garbage truck on Fridays, small Hot Wheels cars that fit perfectly in your hand, grates in the street, planes in the sky, train tracks and choo-choo trains, pygmy goats at the Nature Center, a fascination with monsters, dogs and cats stopping by to visit, piles of sand escaping the sandbox, pretty flowers that do not retain their petals for long, baths with shampoo bottle boats, and lounging on a bench every now and then just to catch your breath. All of these are pieces of you, my young son. Thank you for teaching me to appreciate them, too. journaling 5.10.05, photo 6.5.04

All American
ONE TOUGH KID
U.S.A Born & Raised

ART: JOANNA BOLICK (MASTERS '04)

stitching support

Stitching adds such a lovely textured, homespun look to any layout, but it also adds time to layout production. Stitched Cardstocks from Autumn Leaves (**autumnleaves.com**) give you the stitched look without the effort. By using them, you will convince anyone that you are a needle-wrangling pro. Each pack comes with three unique but coordinated pre-stitched cardstocks. Packs are available in six different themes. Stitches exist in all varieties from zigzag to straight lines. If you're a fan of clean, graphic style, the geometric patterns of these papers will help guide your page design for quick, easy and fabulous layouts. $5.99

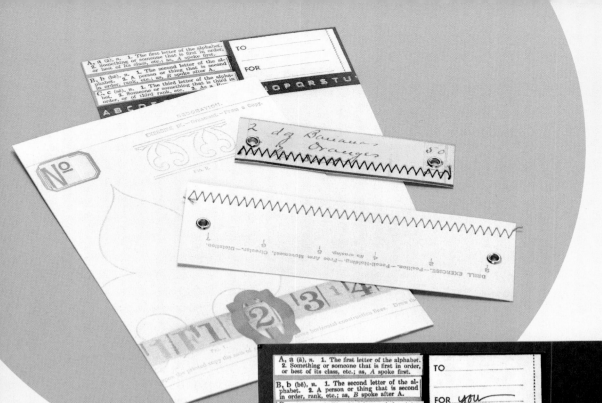

accelerated accents

If you don't have the time (or patience) to re-create the trendy altered style with handmade embellishments, Li'l Davis Designs (**lildavisdesigns.com**) offers Jenni Bowlin Embellished Backgrounds. Jenni incorporates walnut ink, vintage ledger paper, stitching, rickrack and other altered-style staples into each design. The photo-realistic reproductions take out all of the bulk and effort. Each package includes a photo-mat-sized background and two smaller strips for coordinated titles, journaling or captions. $2.99

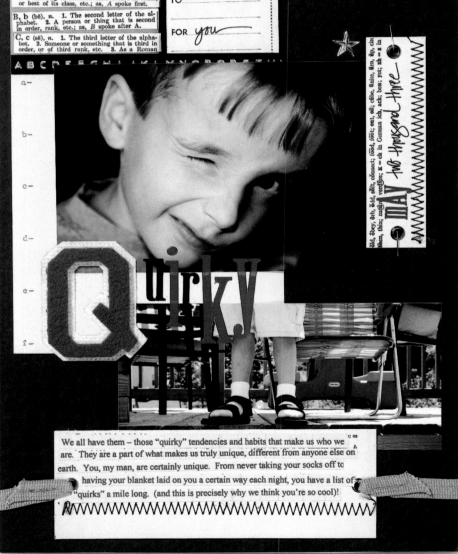

ART: JENNI BOWLIN FOR LI'L DAVIS DESIGNS

immediate inking

There's now a quick and precise way to apply multiple pigment inks to stamps, page edges, stencils or anything else without worrying about cleaning up wandering ink or fussing with time-consuming masks. Delta's (**deltacrafts.com**) new Purecolor inks feature a ½" round sponge tip perfect for precise application of ink on any kind of surface, including glass and metal. Inks come in 24 different shades, including six metallics. $6.99; $7.99 (metallics)

overlay ovation

Me & My Big Ideas (**meandmybigideas .com**) Photo Sleeves were designed for anyone who loves the look of transparency overlays, but struggles with inconspicuous adhesion or tidy trimming. Just match the photo to the proper sleeve size, peel off the self-adhesive backing and stick it to your page. The sleeves are 4 x 4", 4 x 6", or 5 x 7", and each pack offers an assortment of the three sizes. Themes include baby, inspirational, holidays, seasons, sports and school. $4.99

closed

open

hassle-free hinges

Flip Flop Fasteners from Destination Scrapbook Designs (**destinationstickers.com**) give instant flip to elements, allowing for easy interactive page additions to house photos, hidden journaling or any other elements you wish to put on a layout. These self-adhesive clear plastic tabs act as bandage-shaped hinges (see steps below). In contrast to cardstock or metal hinges, they add almost no bulk to your page, can be stacked for multiple layers, are practically invisible and will not wear out at the fold with repeated use. They come in sheets of 82 fasteners in two different sizes (40 small and 42 large). $4

step by step

fast flip books

1. Cut flip pages in desired size from different colors of paper.

2. Use ruler and pencil to mark where you would like the edges of flip pages to rest on the page.

3. Place flip pages so bottom lines up with pencil marks. Adhere with fasteners. Erase pencil marks.

journaling jump-start

Meaningful journaling is often the first thing hurried scrapbookers nix. *Scrapbook Recipes for Journaling* from Hot Off The Press (**paperpizazz.com**) offers "recipes" for fresh ways to get started. It includes suggestions for difficult journaling situations such as sorrowful memories as well as innovative ways to journal. $17.99

If it's simply a journaling prompt you're after, try Stampin' Up (**stampinup.com**) Phrase Starters and Elegant Beginnings stamps. These come in sets of four phrases, and kick in your journaling juice by giving you a starting phrase to complete. They also add a distinct design element to your pages with their fresh and elegant font choices. And, they give you the fun look of stamped titles without having to take the time to stamp each letter individually. $19.95 per set of four

ART: BECKY THOMPSON

ART: PATTY LENNON FOR QUICKUTZ

sticky solutions

Scrapbookers love the look of scripty, detailed fonts that many die-cut machine manufacturers are introducing. But, adhering them to a page is another story. If you are tired of trying to work with messy glues and hard-to-apply adhesives for smaller die-cut shapes and intricate die-cut letters, check out Bazzill Quickstripz from Quickutz (**quickutz.com**). Formulated especially for easing adhesion anxiety for Quickutz fonts, these 12 x 2" strips of textured Bazzill cardstock are self-adhesive and transform anything you cut from them into peel-and-stick paper accents. Quickstripz are available in 15 colors, 10 strips per pack and fit perfectly with the Quickutz hand tool or any other die-cutting tool. They even work well for creating cardstock stickers with your punches and are the perfect size for creating self-sticking die-cut borders. $6.99

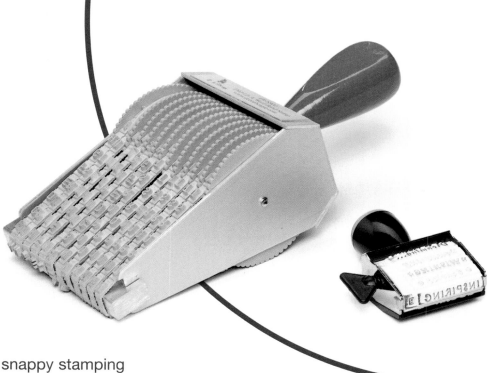

snappy stamping

Mini letter stamps offer cute design and accent possibilities, but they can be a challenge to use. It's hard to feel coordinated when using such tiny tools, and creating straight and evenly spaced words or phrases requires time and patience. With dial-up stamps, perfectly aligned words or phrases can be achieved with the turn of a dial. The Dial-Up a Word stamp from La Pluma (**debrabeagle .com**) allows users to spell their desired sentiment on the stamp by turning the dial. Similarly, La Pluma's Dial-Up a Phrase stamp and Thinkable Inkables from Memories in the Making (**leisurearts.com**) contain phrases or words that can be changed with a quick flip of the dial, and many of the varied font styles are small enough to stamp on things such as twill tape and metal dog tags. Use these tools with any stamp pad for perfect color coordination. Thinkable Inkables (available in 16 themes, 12 phrases to a stamp): $6.99 (Christmas edition, $9.99, also includes ink pad); La Pluma dial-up stamps: $8.99

La Pluma Dial-Up a Word stamp   ART: SUZY WEST

Memories in the Making Thinkable Inkables   ART: SUZY WEST

quick quote-finder

Quote Reference Books from Die Cuts With a View (**diecutswith aview.com**) and their accompanying CD-ROMs make including the perfect quote a snap. The CD-ROM allows you to search the book's quote collection electronically for a specific topic or keyword. Once you've found your quote, copy and paste it right from the computer screen into your digital page or print it out in whatever coordinating color you need. Four books include more than 500 quotes each and are organized by general themes. If you prefer to skip the computer and page through the book, each theme is subdivided into more specific categories to make locating the right quote even quicker. $14.99 per book/CD-ROM set

ART: MICHELLE PESCE (MASTERS '04)

ART: BONNIE BLUMENSTOCK FOR PEBBLES, INC.

easy eyelets

Pebbles, Inc. (**pebblesinc.com**) I kan'dee line has reshaped the traditional eyelet into brad form with Eyelet Brads. This makes using eyelets a two-second process—just push the Eyelet Brad through your paper, fold the legs flat against the backside of your paper, and you have an utterly convincing, perfectly set eyelet. Also, they leave no hole in the middle of your paper.

For the times you do need the hole in the center of the eyelet (for example, to string ribbon or fiber through) but still want a quicker (and quieter) way to set your eyelets, Eyelet Outlet (**eyeletoutlet.com**) introduces the innovative Quicklet. These eyelets can be set with a ball-point pen simply by pushing the pen tip into the back of the eyelet and twisting (see inset, right). No noise. No tools. No hassle. No problem. Eyelet Brads: large $2.99/10 per pack, small $2.49/20 per pack; Quicklets Eyelets: $2.95/84 per pack

step by step

Grandma's BEAUTY

It didn't take long for you to become Grandma's favorite beauty! Being the first granddaughter among two wild and crazy grandsons, I suppose it was expected. And Grandma loves spoiling her baby girl ~ from baby dolls to brand new dresses! But most of all, she loves to spend time with you, and I am so thankful for that. And watching her with you just melts my heart. She has done so much for us over the course of this year, above and beyond anything expected. But that is because your Grandma loves you more than anything in this world, Lillian. This photo of you and Grandma Julie was taken when you were only about six weeks old ~ and already a little beauty! 05-04-05

color wheel RECIPES

Color choices made easy with these classic combinations. by Heather A. Eades

Just like your mother's no-fail sugar cookie recipe, classic color combinations will work everytime. They are just a spin of the color wheel away, making color choices for your pages a breeze. Begin by choosing a color from your photos you'd like to enhance, and then choose one of the basic color recipes from the color wheel to coordinate with the chosen color from your photo. These combinations work best when you use one color as the dominant taste and the others in smaller proportions to spice up your page. The following pages will introduce you to the most common color relationships of complementary, analogous and triadic. Use these color wheel recipes as your guide and discover the joy of cooking up quick colorful pages.

grandma's beauty

Jennifer Bourgeault (Masters '04) borrowed from the recipe files of Mother Nature to whip up this refreshing design. She created a base for this light design using green as the main color and red as the support color. She carried the complementary duo into shimmering accents of ruby red decorative brads and sage green pearlesque buttons.

supplies: Light sage, sage, black and white textured cardstock • Red patterned paper • Silk flowers • Gemstone brads (SEI) • Buttons • Lettering template • Corner rounder • Circle template • Computer font

Complementary

Complementary colors are found directly across from each other on the color wheel. The secret ingredient to a successful complementary-color creation is selecting one color to be dominant and one to be subordinate in the layout. In each complementary pair, there is one warm color and one cool color; so use care in choosing which color will dominate and which will accent the page. The amount of each color utilized will greatly affect the "flavor" of the composition.

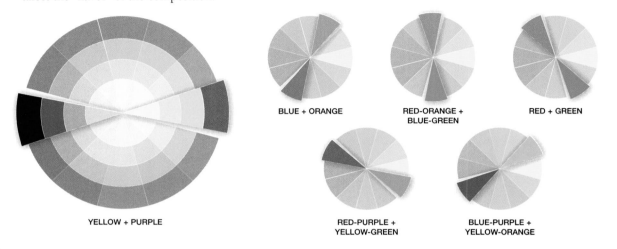

YELLOW + PURPLE

BLUE + ORANGE

RED-ORANGE + BLUE-GREEN

RED + GREEN

RED-PURPLE + YELLOW-GREEN

BLUE-PURPLE + YELLOW-ORANGE

seize the mcmoment

Susan Cyrus (Masters '04) used a large dollop of purple offset by dashes of yellow to commemorate her son's first trip to a Golden Arches' Playland. She pulled from the purple in the photos to fill the right-hand side of the layout, expanding the colors from the images to flow off the page. She leveled off the left side with a mostly yellow photo, which carries up into her title and the smidge of yellow ribbon placed behind the subtitle in the label holder.

supplies: Purple patterned paper (Bo-Bunny) • Purple, white papers • Rub-on words (Déjà Views) • Metal label holder (Magic Scraps) • Bottle caps, bottle cap stickers (Design Originals) • Foam letter stamps (Ma Vinci) • Yellow ribbon • Yellow acrylic paint • Transparency • Foam adhesive • Computer font

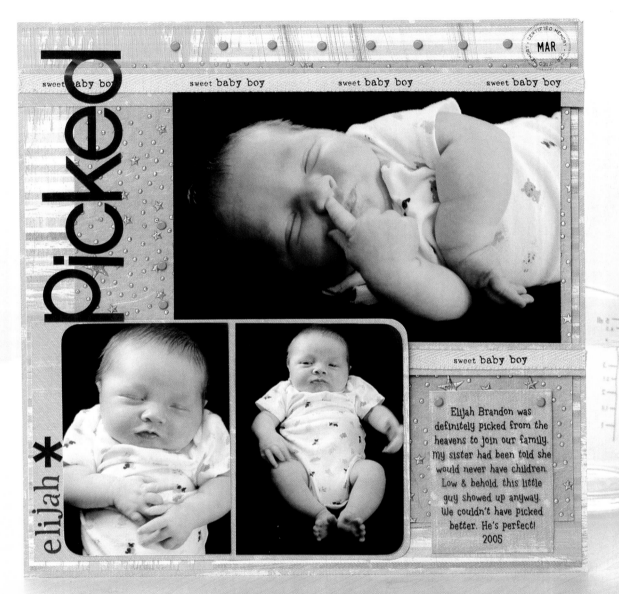

picked

A well-balanced combination of blues and oranges makes this design by Shannon Taylor (Masters '05) a delight to the eyes. Drawing the two complementary colors from the baby's onesie in the photo, Shannon utilized both colors on the layout with patterned paper, orange brads and baby blue printed twill tape. The dashes of blue throughout the layout play nicely off the dominant presence of orange.

supplies: Patterned papers, orange brads (Junkitz) • Decorative star paper (Creative Imaginations) • Printed twill, rub-on date seal (Creative Impressions) • Large letter stickers (American Crafts) • Small letter stickers (Chatterbox) • Leftovers font (downloaded from Internet) • Purple, turquoise, peach, yellow, white papers • Vellum • Rollagraph Summer Days jumbo stamp roller (Clearsnap) • Chalk • Flavia letter stickers (Colorbök) • Computer font • Foam adhesive

Analogous

To whip up a batch of analogous colors, simply select any three colors in consecutive order on the color wheel. To bring out the best in any creation using this color scheme, choose one of the three colors as the main ingredient, one for a complementary flavor and one to garnish. To determine which color will play which role in the mix, consider the final flavor you hope to convey.

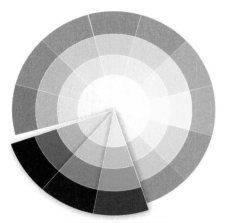

GREEN + BLUE + PURPLE

RED + RED-PURPLE + PURPLE

ORANGE + RED-ORANGE + RED

YELLOW + YELLOW-ORANGE + ORANGE

GREEN + YELLOW-GREEN + YELLOW

BLUE + BLUE-GREEN + GREEN

PURPLE + BLUE-PURPLE + BLUE

one day

Nic Howard (Masters '05) pressed a dreamy, blue-green circle behind her single photo on this page, creating a stargazing, moonlike effect. A complement of blue-purple grounds the layout through a rich and decadent band along the bottom. She poured blue dominantly around the page for unity between the other two support colors. The same blue-green paper used to balance the weight of the photo is also found as a framing background, seasoning the design to her taste.

supplies: Patterned paper (Crafters Workshop, Basicgrey) • Blue, white papers (Bazzill) • Rub-on letters (Making Memories) • Black stamping ink • Computer fonts

ashy's

Using a heaping cup of red-purple on this girlie creation, Kristin Holly of Katy, Texas, added garnishes of red throughout her circle-punched design. A splash of purple ties in the photos and title. Layered hearts act as the title's apostrophe, combining each color involved with this analogous, visual delicacy. The combination of deliciously diva tones simmers with all the fun of being a girl.

supplies: Red, red-purple, purple papers (Doodlebug, Bazzill) • Fiber (Rubba Dub Dub) • Heart, medium circle punches • Large circle punch (Marvy) • Small circle punch (Carl) • Computer font

Ashy's current favorites are (1) Her new Barbie bike, (2) Candy, especially Pez, Sweet Tarts, Nerds and Smarties, and (3) Trips to the Dollar Store! For Easter, Nana and Papa gave her ten dollars to spend on anything and she absolutely loved being able to pick her own treats. She probably would have spent it all on candy if I hadn't intervened though. Her next choice? Jewelry and sparkly accessories! Not sure what's going on, but Ashy's becoming a girlie girl all of a sudden.

Spring 2005

the color **companion**

Stow this cool pocket-sized tool in your crop bag for quickly choosing successful color combinations

This innovative, pocket-sized tool makes color-combining a piece of cake. The Color Companion from C & T Publishing (**ctpub.com**) showcases 24 color schemes on individually numbered cards. Every card highlights one pure hue and reveals its shades (variations of the color made by adding black) and tints (variations of the color made by adding white). The back of each card lists each color's combinations as it is used to create complementary, triadic, analogous and other schemes, along with color-specific usage tips. Developed by noted color expert Joen Wolfrom, the handy color guide is based on the Ives color wheel. $14.95

Triadic

A triadic color scheme is a visual threesome consisting of colors spaced equidistant from each other on the color wheel. Depending on the intensity of the colors you combine, these mixtures can create powerful contrasts or soothing harmonies. Offering more color variety than any other scheme, this combo may be the most difficult to balance. Follow the recipe of using one color as the main ingredient and the other colors in smaller amounts as dashes of flavor. Try subduing one or more colors with a touch of neutrals for success.

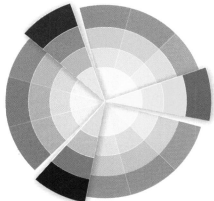

RED + BLUE + YELLOW

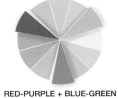

RED-PURPLE + BLUE-GREEN + YELLOW-ORANGE

PURPLE + GREEN + ORANGE

BLUE-PURPLE + YELLOW-GREEN + RED-ORANGE

Here she is...my girl. On New Year's day, to be precise. She had just finished learning how to ride her brand new bike. The light was shining on her hair, making it glow. So pretty. I had to snap a picture.

I have spent a lot of time this year trying to capture Madelyn. See, she is just growing up so fast. She has changed so much this year. Learned to read and to ride her bike. Gained more independence. Became more of her own person.

I find myself constantly trying to catch up with her. Working to figure her out. It's an amazing journey we're on. I hope she just slows down and keeps me along for the ride.

Photo January 2005/Journal May 2005

my girl

Just the right mix of red, yellow and blue are the key ingredients to success on this creation by Tracy Miller of Fallston, Maryland. Inspired by the sweatshirt her daughter is wearing in the photos, Tracy used red as the main ingredient. She rolled out blocks of soft blue and strips of gold to offset her primarily red background. A splash of each color lends flavor to the design. Circle punches combined with patterned paper incorporate all three colors for a visual treat.

supplies: Black, red, dusty blue, mustard, cream papers • Patterned paper • Letter stickers • Spiral stamp • Circle punch • Computer font

may first, the official celebration of thomas birthday. not that attention isn't lavished upon him each day of the year. but his birthday is a guarantee of good things to come. new toys, extra treats and ocean whitefish for his dinner. thomas has been a part of our family for all but 8 weeks of his three years. if i were to blow out his candles and make a wish, i'd hope that he'd be a part of our family for 300 years.

3 T IS THREE

may 2005

t is three

Inspired by the tigerish coat of Thomas the cat in the photo, Melanie Bauer of Columbia, Missouri, chose sassy orange to serve as the main scoop of color on her feline birthday-tribute page. Melanie brings out the bold orange flavor with a paper torn border and a stamped title. A dose of olive green separates the two orange sections, and draws out the cat's eyes as well. The final touch is a dash of purple, displayed in the title block, which spices up the page.

supplies: Olive, violet papers (Bazzill) • Orange patterned paper (Scenic Route) • Rub-on number, tab (Autumn Leaves) • Foam letter stamps

64
no-fail
blueprints

Create quick pages using layout designs from our Masters.

by Sheila Doherty (Masters '05)

Somewhere between taking the kids to school, grocery shopping and working, you've managed to squeeze in a little creative time to scrapbook. You *could* spend all your time trying to figure out how to arrange your layout. Or, you could simply find a blueprint that fits your photos and add your own touch to the design.

When creating a layout from a blueprint, most of the work is done for you. Simply choose a layout to fit your photos, pick out coordinating paper and accents; adhere everything into place and you're done.

Have a horizontal photo but want to use a blueprint that has the focal photo in a vertical position? Just give the blueprint a turn. There are unlimited ways to view just one blueprint, such as by rotating or reversing it (see right).

In the following pages, our Masters offer a bundle of their own blueprints to make your scrapbooking quicker.

discover
unlimited layout variations within one blueprint:

rotate right

reverse (flip)

rotate180

rotate left, flip

3 photos to 4

accent in lieu of a photo

Apply any of these variances to a blueprint to multiply the ideas.

KEY

P = Photos
J = Journaling
TITLE = Page Title

Catch
of the day

It took a lot of courage on my part to relax around the water and just let the kids fish to their hearts content. Jacob quickly learnt about the fishing rod, baiting, dropping the line in and catching the fish. He was extremely proud of this 'slimy mackrel' as his Dad called it. He pulled it in and insisted we keep it to smoke when we got home. When we arrived back to the bach, we took the obligatory fish photos. Paul prepared it, while Jacob sorted his fishing rod out. It was, by far, the biggest fish caught that weekend.

11:1 JAN 2005

catch of the day

This 3-photo blueprint works well to tell a fishtale by Nic Howard (Masters '05). The focal photo shows off her son's big catch while the two support photos matted with aged tags tell more about the proud moment. The tags are topped with fishing swivels strung on fishing line that is wrapped around a portion of the background. The rough orange background paper complements the masculine photos.

supplies: Blue paper • Patterned papers (Basicgrey, 7 Gypsies, Paper Loft) • Brown stamping ink (Clearsnap) • Preserve It de-acidification spray (Krylon) • Rub-ons (Making Memories) • Fishing swivels • Bambi Bold font (typenow.net) • Tahoma font (myfonts.com)

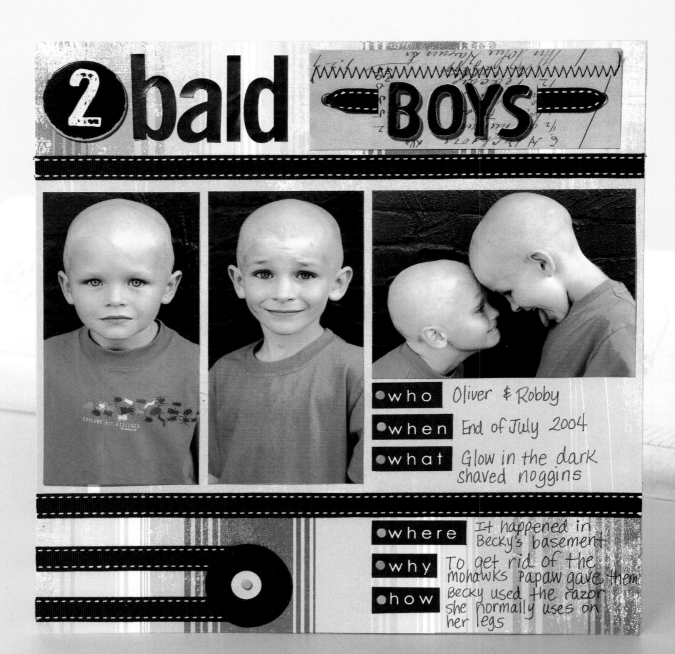

two bald boys
Choosing headshots of each of her sons for the vertical photos and one of them acting silly together for the one horizontal photo, Shannon Taylor (Masters '05) expertly utilized the blueprint for this layout. She adds a little punch to her title by using various premade alphabets. Stickers act as journaling prompts, which are finished with handwritten answers to the questions.

supplies: Patterned papers (Basicgrey) • Orange tag, chipboard number (Li'l Davis) • Letter stickers (American Crafts) • Paper Bliss wooden letters (Westrim) • Phrase stickers (Chatterbox) • Zig pen (EK Success) • Brads (Junkitz) • Ribbon • Eyelets

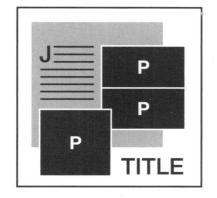

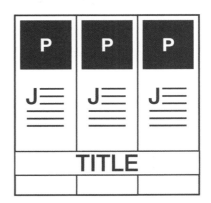

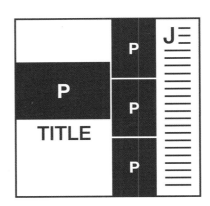

By glancing at this page you may think it is about our visit to the Minneapolis sculpture gardens - but, it is not.

I think jordan is finally starting to understand my obsession. Most of the time she thinks I am crazy for taking tons of photos and spending countless hours scrapbooking them.

Before we got to the garden, we stopped at a scrapbook store. jordan talked me into buying her a

little round CD tin/mini scrapbook. I bought it for her knowing full-well that she would never do anything with it.

Then out of nowhere, she got it. She started snapping pictures and talking about how she was going to scrap them in her new little tin.

So there you have it, this layout is to document the place and day when jordan entered into my crazy and creative world of scrapbooking.

Minneapolis Sculpture Garden
May 7th 2005

minneapolis, mn

Jodi Heinen (Masters '05) picked a strong horizontal photo of the Minneapolis Sculpture Gardens as a perfect focal point for this four-photo blueprint documenting the day her daughter started to "get" scrapbooking. Her title and accents all reinforce the circle theme suggested by the circular photos. If desired, the circular photos could be made into square or rectangular photos or even embellishments to suit the scrapbooker's needs.

supplies: Green, red papers • Lollipop Shoppe paper, letter stickers (Basicgrey) • Tags (Making Memories) • Letter stickers (Chatterbox) • Jolee's Boutique spoon charm (EK Success) • Brads (Bazzill) • Ribbon (Offray) • Roxie, Unconventional fonts (twopeasinabucket.com)

time for the
GUN SHOW

Do you have any tape?
'Cause I'm RIPPED!
Do you have a band-aid?
'Cause I'm CUT!
Do you have any bullets?
...For my GUNS!

Liane was home from college for the week.
It was 9 p.m., dinner was over, and the wine bottle was empty.
So she decided to entertain us.
A nationally ranked swimmer, she's got nice biceps.
And that night, we learned just how much she loved them.
Really, how can you blame her? Those are some sweet guns!

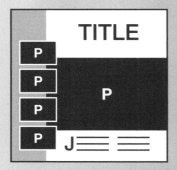

time for the gun show

Bright, colorful papers are fitting for this layout by Jessie Baldwin (Masters '05), playing up the silliness of these photos of her swimmer sister showing off her biceps. Instead of keeping the title contained in its box, the title overlaps the top of the focal photo. This blueprint as well as the variations prove an enlarged photo and several cropped support photos can fit comfortably on one layout.

supplies: Blue, yellow papers (Prism) • Uptown patterned paper (Cross-My-Heart) • Letter stickers (American Crafts) • Stazon solvent ink (Tsukineko) • Abadi MT Condensed font (designgraphics.org) • Times New Roman font (fonts.com)

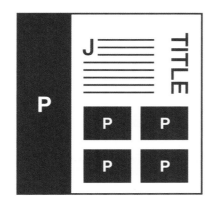

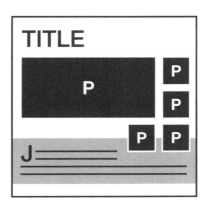

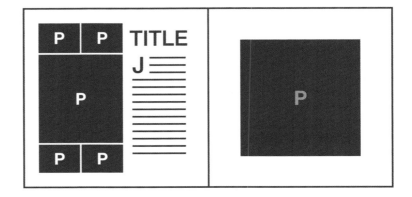

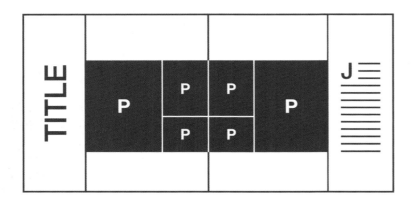

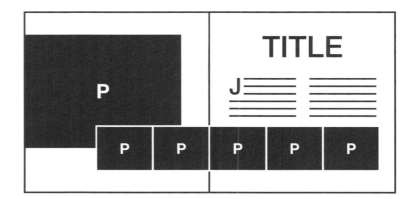

"A penny for your thoughts."
A phrase that I have heard
a million times. It wasn't
until now that I realize what
it really means. I look at you
sometimes, and I can't believe
how much you've grown. You
have a mind of your own, and
sometimes I have to stop in
my tracks because I can't
believe it. My little guy isn't
so little anymore.

August 2004

your · thoughts

your thoughts

In this clean and colorful layout, Julie Johnson (Masters '05) reflects on how quickly her son is growing up. The focal photo displays the inspiration for Julie's page title, while the horizontal line of the top five photos allows for easy comparison of the different expressions of her son's face. Julie chose to strengthen the horizontal lines suggested by the blueprint by adding bold, striped ribbons across the page.

supplies: Orange, black, blue papers (Prism) • Patterned paper (Daisy D's) • Vellum • Ribbon (Making Memories) • Colorbox Fluid Chalk stamping ink (Clearsnap) • Pennies • Staples

stolen moments

Jenn Brookover (Masters '05) used this blueprint to create a bright photo collage of her son. The design lends itself well to the various angles and close-up shots of her son and the items he is wearing. The colors in the photos are repeated in the circular accents, patterned paper and the title. "Since my blueprint showed me exactly where to put my title and journaling, I didn't have to mess around with where everything was going to go...I could just create!" Jenn explains.

supplies: Letter stickers, blue, striped patterned papers (KI Memories) • Circle patterned paper (Scenic Route) • Light blue paper (Bo-Bunny) • Letter stickers (Doodlebug) • Boy stickers (7 Gypsies) • Tiny letter stickers (Making Memories) • Headache font (downloaded from the Internet)

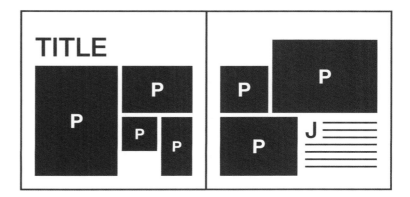

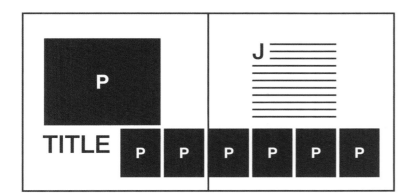

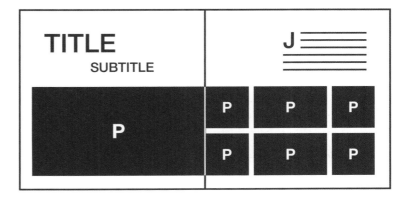

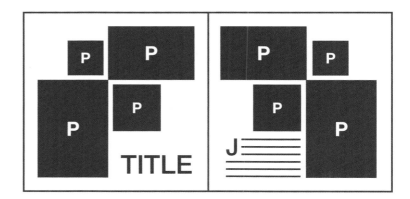

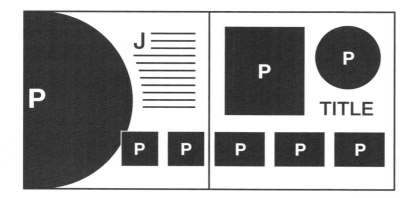

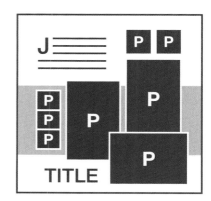

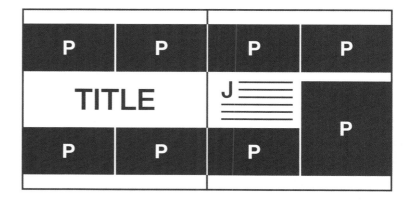

With so much to do, Legoland was a delightful way to spend a summer day. Not only were the Lego animals & buildings fun to look at, but there was never an end of rides & attractions just for kids your size. The two biggest hits were the Dino Dig, where you got to dig for dinosaur bones in the sand, & the cars, where you each got to drive the car of your choice all by yourselves. Having Catherine & Grandmother along just made the day even more special. We all had such a great time we came back the following week to do it all again.

June 2004

play day

Sheila Doherty (Masters '05) documented a day at Legoland with her children and her niece in this 8-photo layout. Sheila added two wide blocks of patterned paper to the design of this layout as well as a red border to the edges to balance the multitude of colors in the photos. The blueprint allowed Sheila to easily fit a lot of photos on her layout and not worry about forgetting to leave room for the journaling and title.

supplies: Patterned papers (Scenic Route, Imagination Project) • Red, green papers • Letter stickers (KI Memories) • Button (Colorbök) • Concho (Scrapworks) • Rub-ons (Imagination Project) • Metal clip (Scrappin' Ware) • Orange ribbon (American Crafts) • Century Gothic font (linotype.com) • Metal stitched square, mini brads, yellow button (Making Memories)

haunted hayloft

Detailing the newest spooky Halloween tradition in their household, Christine Brown (Masters '05) shares how each of her sons approached the Haunted Hayloft. Distressed papers in fall colors play up the Halloween theme of this layout. In her interpretation of the blueprint, Christine matted the small outside photos with walnut-inked tags.

supplies: Striped patterned paper (Scenic Route) • Cream paper (Paper Loft) • Brown paper (Pebbles) • Tags (7 Gypsies) • Twill (Creative Impressions) • Fabric letters (Making Memories) • Sonnets letter stickers (Creative Imaginations) • Yellow letter stickers (Karen Foster) • Inspirables Alpha Stones (EK Success) • Suede font (scrapvillage.com) • Airplane font (twopeasinabucket.com)

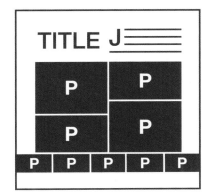

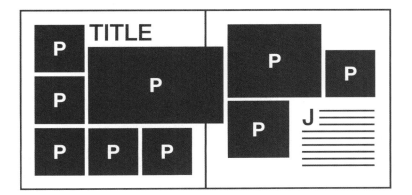

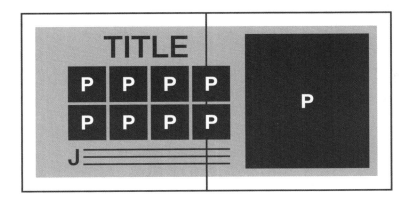

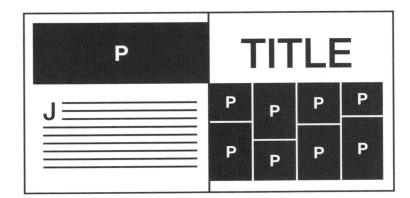

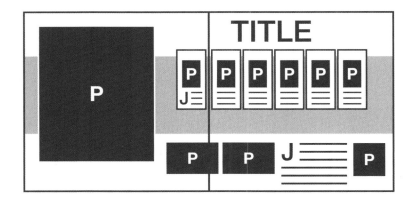

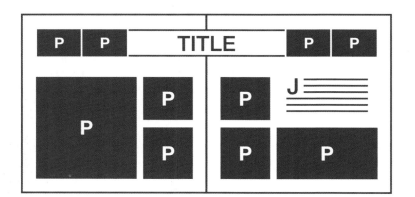

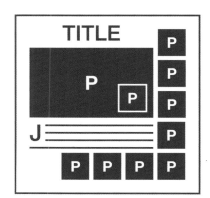

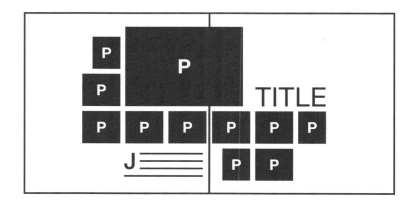

What A Weekend!

Wow! What a weekend! QuicKutz brought all ten members of their design team to Utah for a weekend of shopping, dining, and pampering. Each of the members of the team taught a mini class and we came away with a great keepsake album. My favorite part of the trip was probably touring the manufacturing plant where they make the dies. QuicKutz has been an amazing company to work with and I feel very blessed to be a part of their team.

Top to Bottom:
Patty Lennon
Libby Weifenbach
Jen Sizemore
Jennifer Miller
Lisa LeClair
Polly McMillan
Holle Wiktorek
Meredith Holman
Samantha VanArnhem

what a weekend

This 10-photo blueprint is a perfect fit for Kelli Noto's (Masters '03) layout about the ladies she met on a scrapbook retreat. She matted a small photo of each woman with pink paper and set apart the group shot by framing it with gingham ribbon and a bow. The green horizontal stripe for the title and the vertical argyle stripe for the journaling help to balance the photos on the opposite side of the layout. Small photos work great for small detail shots or headshots, while the larger photos can give an overall view of an event.

supplies: Patterned paper (Carolee's Creations) • Ginger die-cut alphabet (Quickutz) • Clear mailing label (3M) • Ribbon • Eyelets

Changing
LIKE THE
Seasons

September

October

November

August

June

July

• born 6.11.01
• Baptism 7.29.01
• sweet, sleepy, ♥
  snuggly newborn

SUMMER

fall

• rolling over
• sitting up
• big bathtub

winter
◦ first Christmas
◦ loving the jumper
◦ 1st Valentines ♡

December

January

February

March

April

May

spring
• first swing
• crawling
• 1st Disney trip

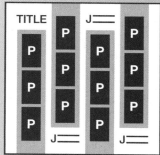

changing like the seasons

A 12-photo blueprint lends itself well to detailing 12 months of the year. For each month, Jeniece Higgins (Masters '05) included a photo of her son during that month of his life, showing in one layout how much he changed from month to month. The photos were all changed to black-and-white to unify the photos and remove clashing colors. Each line of photos was then matted with pastel strips, keeping with the baby theme.

supplies: Cream paper (Bazzill) • Handmade papers (Provo Craft) • Rub-ons (Li'l Davis, Doodlebug, Kopp) • Flowers, leaves (Prima) • Date stamp (Making Memories) • Versacolor, Stazon stamping inks (Tsukineko) • Notebook paper • Staples • Charm • Watercolor pencil

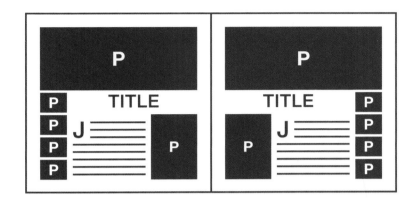

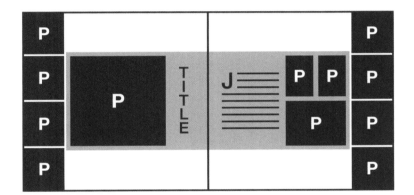

simplify it

Get the detailed look without all the fuss. by Julie Labuszewski and Trisha McCarty-Luedke

You've seen and admired them in Memory Makers magazines and books—those oh-so beautiful pages that seem oh-so time-consuming. Don't be intimidated—be inspired. You can create the look of a detailed page by making a few quick and easy choices. By taking an easier route, nine artists captured the look and feel of previously published complex layouts in half the time. Learn about their fast and easy solutions to labor-intensive and time-consuming designs.

original

ART: KARI HANSEN
"FABRIC FASCINATIONS," P. 74, OCTOBER 2004

fall leaves

A close look at the fall page designed by Kelli Noto (Masters '03) reveals quick and easy design solutions to the original layout by Kari Hansen, craft editor. Kelli captured the rich fall textures of fabric by layering patterned paper instead. "Mixing patterned paper can be intimidating, but I knew that if I stayed as close to Kari's choices as I could, I would be safe," Kelli says. Kelli preserved the feel of fall photos that Kari printed on twill fabric by cutting and matting leaf photo stickers. Pre-threaded, self adhesive buttons are a quick alternative to hand-covered fabric buttons. Printing journaling onto gold vellum is a shortcut to painting the back of a transparency.

supplies: Patterned papers (Daisy D's, Scenic Route) • Vellum • Stickers (Pebbles) • Die-cut letters (Quickutz) • Self-adhesive buttons (EK Success) • Twill tape

original effect:	simplified shortcut:
hand-covered fabric buttons	pre-threaded, self-adhesive buttons
photos printed on twill fabric	photo stickers
handcut title	die-cut title
frayed fabric	paper strips

simplified

Fall in Colorado is such a wonderful time. It is often a short-lived season, as the colorful leaves will disappear after the first snow. This fall happened to be milder and the colors hung around for a bit longer. We don't have the overly colorful falls here because most of the trees are cottonwoods and only turn yellow, but it is still a magical time. We take advantage of the season by walking more and taking longer bike rides. This picture was taken at Delany Farm, one of our favorite places, when Eric was six.

simplified

original

ART: KARI HANSEN
"BOHEMIAN RHAPSODY," P. 62, FEBRUARY 2005

patience

Elizabeth Ruuska of Rensselaer, Indiana, designed a page just as luxurious as the one by Kari Hansen, craft editor, but in a simpler fashion. The lavish textures Kari achieved with layered ribbons are carried through on Elizabeth's page by using strips of tapestry patterned papers. The sparkly effect of hand-strung beads is made simple with the use of metallic fiber. Pre-threaded, self-adhesive buttons are a quick fix to hand-sewn ones. Elizabeth also saved time using stickers instead of real buckles and hinges. Journaling printed on gold vellum is a timesaver to painting the back of a transparency. "I think it still looks good with all the shortcuts," says Elizabeth. "Definitely faster and less expensive, too."

supplies: Patterned papers (Anna Griffin, K & Co., Reminisce) • Paper strip border (Mini Graphics) • Distress Ink (Ranger) • Sonja letter dies (Quickutz) • Clock charm • Buckle, label holder stickers • Fibers • Evening Stroll font (Autumn Leaves) • Viviana font (downloaded from the Internet)

original effect:	simplified shortcut:
rows of ribbons	patterned paper strips
buckles & hinges	buckle & hinges stickers
paint behind transparency	print journaling on gold vellum
handcut title	die cut title
hand-threaded beads	metallic fiber
hand-sewn buttons	pre-threaded buttons

ART: JENIECE HIGGINS (MASTERS '05)
"MEET THE MASTERS," P. 89, FEBRUARY 2005

i love you the best

Jennifer Bourgeault (Masters '04) enjoyed the freedom of taking the page design by Jeniece Higgins (Masters '05) and making it her own with a few shortcuts. Jennifer preserved the tattered look of frayed fabrics by tearing a mix of patterned papers. Instead of tenaciously adhering ribbon, Jennifer used ribbonlike stickers. In place of label holders adhered with brads, she used label holder stickers. Inking the edges is a shortcut to dimension rather than sewing.

supplies: Purple, plaid patterned papers (Karen Foster) • Embossed paper • Floral vellum • Vellum • Self-adhesive buttons (EK Success) • Ribbon stickers (Mrs. Grossman's) • Label holder stickers (Creek Bank) • Letter stickers (Creative Imaginations, Wordsworth, C.R. Gibson) • Black stamping ink • Computer fonts

original effect:	simplified shortcut:
frayed fabric	torn paper
label holders with brads	label holder stickers
stitched edges	inked edges
fabric	patterned paper
ribbon	ribbon stickers

ART: MICHELLE MINKEN
"FABRIC FASCINATIONS," P. 69, FEBRUARY 2005

remnants of rome

The essence of the collage page by Michelle Minken, marketing manager, is captured in less time by Joanna Bolick (Masters '04). "There are so many layers to Michelle's design that it was fun to experiment with different patterns to achieve something similar," says. To simplify the process, Joanna used patterned papers instead of fabric remnants, which can be time-consuming to adhere. To create the stitched look, she used rub-on stitches. Joanna chose a font for her title that resembled stitched lines then printed it on a transparency—a quicker choice than Michelle's hand-stitched title. The effect of an embroidered letter is achieved with a twill tape letter.

supplies: Patterned papers (My Mind's Eye, 7 Gypsies, Making Memories, Design Originals, Anna Griffin, Memories Complete, Déjà Views by C-Thru Ruler, K & Co.) • Transparency • Rub-on stitches (Sew Easy, Doodlebug, My Mind's Eye) • Ribbon • Pearls • Twill letters (Carolee's Creations) • Labels (Me & My Big Ideas) • Folio closure (Colorbök) • Rome sticker (Design Originals) • Anna Griffin frames (Plaid) • Mini letter stickers • Laser-cut lace (Cardeaux) • Canvas paper (Fredrix) • Label holder • Frazzled font (Autumn Leaves)

original effect:	simplified shortcut:
hand-stitched title	stitchlike font
layered fabric	layered patterned paper
stitching	rub-on stitches
stitched lace	adhered paper lace
embroidered letter	twill tape letter
hand-sewn buttons	self-adhesive folio closures

original

ART: DEBI BORING
"15 GREAT STAMPED BACKGROUNDS,"
SCRAPBOOKING AND STAMPING, P. 46, WINTER 2005

beach babes

Amy Goldstein of Kent Lakes, New York, achieved the detailed look of serendipity-squares shown on Debi Boring's page but in less time. "I cut patterned paper into squares instead of tearing and stamping a collage," Amy says. "It took a tenth of the time." After inking the edges of the 1⅝" squares, Amy adhered them to the background. For additional serendipity effects, she stamped beach motifs on blocks of tan speckled paper. A premade frame is a quick solution to a collaged slide mount.

supplies: Tan, turquoise, striped papers (Junkitz) • Shell, collage patterned papers (Design Originals) • Chipboard frame (Li'l Davis) • Snaps, brads (Junkitz) • Letter stickers (NRN) • Sand dollar stamp (Club Scrap) • Starfish stamp (Mostly Animals) • Ribbon (Offray)

simplified

original effect:	simplified shortcut:
torn-paper and stamped collage	patterned paper
collaged slide mount	premade frame
shell accents	quick-tie accent
printed title	sticker title

simplified

Our hearts are linked together by a love only a mother and daughter can share; a bond that goes way beyond any words; a feeling of togetherness that goes very deep in our hearts. I know that no matter how big you get and where you end up in this life our hearts will always be linked together in this very special way.

original

ART: DIANA HUDSON (MASTERS '03)
HARDWARE STORE FINDS, P. 59, MARCH/APRIL 2004

linked by love

A quick and easy mindset allowed Heather Preckel of Swannanoa, North Carolina, to create a simplified but just as farm-fresh layout as the page by Diana Hudson (Masters '03). Filled with hardware store embellishments such as chicken wire and hinges, Diana's page took time to assemble. Heather found a timesaving solution with sticker hinges. And even though she skipped using chicken wire or gingham and toile fabrics, Heather still captured a homespun feel with gingham and chicken patterned papers. In lieu of a painted and sanded corrugated cardboard frame, Heather cut a frame from pre-distressed patterned paper and then raised it with dimensional adhesive. Instead of handmade fabric covered buttons, premade buttons are adhered in a snap.

supplies: Patterned papers (Rusty Pickle, Daisy D's, Scenic Route, C.R. Gibson) • Buttons (Junkitz) • Dee's Designs sticker hinges (My Mind's Eye) • Tags (7 Gypsies) • Stamping ink (Ranger) • Game board letters (Making Memories) • Wooden letters (Westrim) • Ribbon

original effect:	simplified shortcut:
metal hinges	sticker hinges
fabric	patterned paper
painted & sanded paper	crackle patterned paper
handmade fabric-covered buttons	premade buttons

your guide to **shortcuts**

Try these quick substitutions in lieu of time-involved embellishing.

effect:	shortcut:
for the finished look of handmade fabric-covered and hand-sewn buttons	use pre-threaded, self-adhesive buttons or self-adhesive folio closures
for the textural effect of fabric	use patterned, embossed and textured papers
for customized handcut titles	try using letter die cuts, stickers, rub-ons or stamps
for the worn look of frayed fabric	tear paper
for the look of label holders adhered with brads	use label-holder stickers
for the definition of stitched edges	ink paper edges
for accenting with ribbon	use ribbon stickers
for metal accents	try faux metal stickers
for enhancing words printed on a transparency by painting behind it	print journaling onto colored vellum
for the sparkly effect of micro beads	accent with metallic fibers, metallic paint pen, metallic paper or a metallic ink pad
for the detailed look of a hand-stitched or embroidered title	print your journaling in a stitchlike font
for the definition of stitching or a quilted look	try rub-on stitches, drawing lines with a pen and inking edges with an ink pad
for the handmade touch of embroidered letters	try twill tape letters
for the mixed look of collage	use a collage patterned paper
for the look of a stamped word or accent	use a phrase or accent rub-on
for the look of metal hinges	apply sticker hinges
for the distressed effects using paint, sandpaper and walnut-ink	use pre-distressed products or lend an aged look with the brush of a brown ink pad
for the look of a handmade frame	use a premade frame or a photo mat
for the look of a handmade tag	use a premade, pre-embellished tag
for the look of handcut shapes	use punches, die cuts and stickers

die-cut title

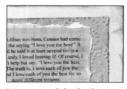

torn paper, inked edges

faux metal stickers

stitchlike font, rub-on stitches

collage patterned paper

sticker hinges

premade frame, pre-distressed products

reader
idea
gallery

45 new page ideas organized
by the fast-and-easy techniques
listed below

Free Spirit
Joanna Bolick (Masters '04)

The engaging green and purple color combination lets the vibrancy of this photo shine. Joanna layered strips of paper with ribbon, highlighting them with paper flowers and rhinestones. Her journaling and title were printed on a transparency and placed over patterned vellum.

supplies: Purple paper, flower, ribbon (Making Memories) • Patterned paper (Rusty Pickle) • Vellum (Autumn Leaves) • Word plaque (Li'l Davis) • Rhinestone brads (SEI) • Transparency • Handcrafted, Constitution fonts (Autumn Leaves) • Times font (linotype.com)

Free
Spirit

As the sun set on this warm summer's day, Lindsey began to dance before us. It was wonderful to see her filled with such youthful exuberance, unencumbered by any worries or cares. I treasure these moments of innocence in her life and hope that she'll always be free to dance, laugh, and live life to its fullest extent.

July 2005

remember

PHOTO: ALLISON ORTHNER

My Treasure

Linda Albrecht, St. Peter, Minnesota

The rustic accents on this page match the earthy background. Linda cut flowers from a piece of patterned paper and secured them to the layout with rivets. For the title, she enhanced premade tags with rub-ons, a stencil and paper flowers, using safety pins to hang the tags from buttonhole twill tape. To create the background, Linda layered blocks and strips of papers patterned with stripes, daisy motifs, plaid and text.

supplies: Patterned paper, premade tag, stencil, rub-ons, photo corners, rivets, Monument font (Chatterbox) • Patterned paper, buttonhole twill tape (Carolee's Creations) • Safety pins (Making Memories) • Transparency

A Day With M

Angelia Wigginton
Belmont, Mississippi

A few simple accents are used to create a fun page about a typical day with a young girl. Angelia pieced her papers together and embellished one side with feminine decorative trim. She traced an oversized letter onto patterned paper to create the giant monogram, which she dressed up with printed twill tape and a charm.

supplies: Patterned paper, embossed paper, letter stickers (SEI) • Epoxy letters, rub-on (Li'l Davis) • Oversized letter (My Mind's Eye) • Printed twill (7 Gypsies) • Braided trim (Me & My Big Ideas) • Heart charm • Hemp • Typewriter font (free-typewriter-fonts.com)

Walking the Dog

Beverly Sizemore, Sulligent, Alabama

Beverly used simple flower die cuts to accent her page and coordinate with her patterned paper. She allowed the patterned paper to inspire the colors of the accents and matching title element. The paint chip creates a vibrant background for her title, which she further embellished with eyelets to coordinate with the page.

supplies: Blue, white papers (Bazzill, National Cardstock) • Patterned paper, acrylic charms, eyelets (Doodlebug) • Alphabet stamps (Purple Onion) • Stamping ink (Clearsnap) • Rub-ons (Making Memories) • Ribbon (Offray) • Flower dies (Quickutz) • Paint chip • Foam adhesive • 1942 Report font (momscorner4kids.com)

Allison

Vicki Harvey, Champlin, Minnesota

Three simple accents were all that was needed to make this page pop. Vicki painted a metal tin and used a letter stencil as a mask to create the "A." The large silk flower adds a decidedly girly touch, and Vicki attached a button to its center. A blue tapestry ribbon helps break up and anchor the page as well as add a splash of exciting color.

supplies: Peach paper (Bazzill) • Patterned paper (Daisy D's) • Ribbon • Alphabet stamps (Hero Arts) • Stamping ink (Stampin' Up) • Artistic Expressions tin accent (Autumn Leaves) • Foam stamp, date stamps (Making Memories) • Paint (Delta) • Metallic rub-ons (Craf-T) • Letter stencil (Hunt) • Varnish • Flower (Michaels) • Button • Pegsanna font (downloaded from the Internet)

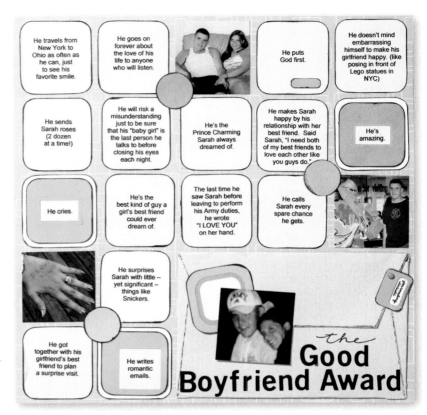

The Good Boyfriend Award

Amanda Goodwin
Munroe Falls, Ohio

Amanda's page design centers on short journaling captions that she housed in small rounded squares. They are filled with reasons why her friend's boyfriend is so worthy of such an honor. To accent the page and draw attention to specific journaling captions, Amanda used colorful paper slide mounts. These and the other page accents—a few circles, a tag and a brad—provide effective spot color.

supplies: Gray paper (Bazzill) • Patterned paper, premade accents (KI Memories) • Brad (Making Memories) • Stamping ink (Tsukineko) • Zig pen (EK Success) • Stickers (American Crafts)

Elsie

Elsie Bustamante
Chula Vista, California

Knotted strands of ribbon draw attention to and anchor journaling captions on this page. In the captions, Elsie used poignant quotes to define the various roles in her life—wife, mother and teacher. She let the plaid patterned paper dictate her color scheme, choosing greens and plum as the dominant and secondary colors, respectively, and saving pink to use as the accent color.

supplies: Plum, pink papers (Bazzill) • Patterned paper (Daisy D's) • Ribbon, rub-on letters (Making Memories) • Eyelet brads (Pebbles) • Button (Junkitz) • Transparency • Arial font (fonts.com)

10 Reasons

Susan Weinroth
Centerville, Minnesota

These playful strip captions list the top 10 reasons why Susan's dog Toby has a great life. She focuses on his daily activities, listing everything from stereotypical dog behavior to items original to Toby. She printed each listing on paper, cut them into strips and inked the edges. Susan used numbered labels and tiles to further embellish each strip.

supplies: Green, tan papers (Bazzill) • Patterned paper, letter stickers (KI Memories) • Alphabet stamps (Ma Vinci's) • Colorbox stamping ink (Clearsnap) • Flower, brad, rub-ons (Making Memories) • Label maker (Dymo) • Tiles (Magic Scraps) • Computer fonts (Chatterbox)

Just Me

Susan Weinroth
Centerville, Minnesota

Susan not only packs this page with specific details, she also used her journaling strips as design elements. Each caption is an example of a trade-mark characteristic. She attached them to the page with rhinestone brads along two border strips she created by machine stitching across the top and bottom of the photo. The white strips add a bright break to the muted and distressed colors of the background.

supplies: White paper (Bazzill) • Patterned papers (Basicgrey) • Rhinestone brads (SEI) • Ribbon (May Arts) • Silk flower • Letter stickers (American Crafts) • Thread • Computer font

Friends

Brandi Barnes, Kelso, Tennessee

Colorful serendipity squares make up a border to balance this photo. Brandi used punched squares of patterned papers, stickers, eyelets, ribbon, acrylic accents, tiny photos and more to create them. Serendipity squares are a great way to use scraps or forgotten-about supplies. Look for colors and styles that coordinate, grab a square punch and create fun accents.

supplies: Pink paper (Bazzill) • Patterned papers (KI Memories, American Crafts, 7 Gypsies) • Stickers (Sonnets by Creative Imaginations, Pebbles, Frances Meyer) • Page pebble, ribbon charms, brads (Making Memories) • Label maker (Dymo) • Rub-ons (Royal & Langnickel) • Acrylic letters (Doodlebug) • Ribbon (Offray) • Metal flower (Carolee's Creations) • Metal accent (Marcella by Kay) • Friendship charm (Darice) • Eyelets • Computer font

Unbearably Cute

Sandra Hicks, San Antonio, Texas

Most children befriend a stuffed bear, and this torn paper bear is a charming accent to show that friendship. Sandra created this paper accent by tearing tan paper into shapes to resemble the bear. She chalked the paper and added a chalked paper flower to match the one resting atop the bear in the photo.

supplies: Blue, green papers, chalk (EK Success) • Patterned paper (Creative Imaginations) • Alphabet stamps, stamping ink (Stampin' Up) • Flowers, ribbon (Making Memories) • Brads (Provo Craft) • Computer font

All Things Pink

Shelley Rankin
Fredericton, New Brunswick, Canada

Large letters make fashionable design elements. For this page, Shelley used a huge "P" to emphasize her daughter's love of pink. She reverse-printed the letter twice (one a size smaller) to use as a guide. After tracing both on deep pink and salmon papers, she cut them out with a craft knife and then layered them. She embellished the smaller of the two with patterned paper. The flower element was handcut from paper and embellished with a sticker. Its stem was created by stapling twill tape to the letter.

supplies: Pink paper • Patterned papers (KI Memories, Anna Griffin, Me & My Big Ideas, K & Co.) • Rub-ons, brads (Scrapworks) • Ribbon, metal letters (Making Memories) • 3-D FX accent stickers (American Traditional) • Nick Bantock stamping ink (Ranger)

Almost Pals

Danielle Thompson, Tucker, Georgia

The crescent strips Danielle cut from patterned paper both accent the page and act as a design element. The overall curve of the border gives a subtle framing effect to the photos. She covered a wooden star with various letter stickers and attached it to her page, connecting the arching strips of paper.

supplies: Patterned papers (Fancy Pants, Arctic Frog, Anna Griffin) • Leather flower (Making Memories) • Letter stickers (Basicgrey, Paper Loft, Pebbles, Creative Imaginations) • Wooden star • Buttons (Blumenthal Lansing, Wal-Mart, Junkitz) • Weathervane font (twopeasinabucket.com)

My Little Rascal

Marla Kress, Cheswick, Pennsylvania

Inspired by the quilted pattern in the lower edge of the photo, Marla mixed patterned papers for this layered and stitched background. The papers come from a coordinated line, and Marla stitched them at the seams with a zig-zag pattern. She used a craft knife to cut her title from patterned paper.

supplies: Black paper • Patterned papers, stickers, tags (Basicgrey) • Ribbon • Frame charms (Leave Memories) • Computer font

Tyler & Karly

Kimberly Brock, Maineville, Ohio

Blocks cut from scraps of patterned paper and placed at angles along the bottom of the page create a border full of summer fun. Kimberly continues the fun by matting an enlarged photo on patterned paper and echoing the strips at the top left of the page. A pair of flip-flops leave footprints by the title in the form of micro-bead "puddles."

supplies: Orange paper (Bazzill) • Patterned papers (KI Memories) • Conchos (Scrapworks) • Brads (Karen Foster) • Ribbon (May Arts) • Rub-ons, flower (Making Memories) • Epoxy sticker (K & Co.) • Embossing template (Lasting Impressions) • Cork stickers (Creative Imaginations) • Versacolor watermark ink (Tsukineko) • Art Accentz beads (Provo Craft) • Clear gloss medium

Joy

Miki Benedict, Modesto, California

Contrasting patterns of bold stripes, sparse polka dots and playful circles highlight this joyful photo. Miki accented various small square accents with patterned and solid ribbons. Struck by the joy her son brings to everyone around him, Miki wrote a heartfelt note to him, adding an acrylic word for punch.

supplies: Blue paper (Bazzill) • Patterned paper, labels, epoxy square (KI Memories) • Sonnets letter stickers (Creative Imaginations) • Joy flashcard (Weathered Door) • Déjà Views rub-ons (C-Thru Ruler) • Ribbon

Meagan

Tania Duczak
Montreal, Quebec, Canada

A strip of patterned paper grounds this layout by stretching out across the bottom third of the page. To add a bit of contrast, Tania tore a piece of the same patterned paper, gave it a quarter turn and adhered it so it angled against the vertical stripes of the original piece, creating the look of a mitred corner. She accented the paper with ribbon and used a premade quote along the side to create a border.

supplies: Green, peach papers (Bazzill) • Patterned paper, stickers (All My Memories) • Versacolor ink (Tsukineko) • Ribbon (Die Cuts With a View) • Flower, metal letter (Making Memories) • Americana font (myfonts.com)

My Greatest Love

Catherine Mathews-Scanlon
Middletown, Rhode Island

Layered lines of stitching ring this page's top, right and bottom sides to create a pocket that holds the journaling of Catherine's emotional journey that took place after the birth of her son. Catherine created her page and ran it under her sewing machine a few times to create these imperfect lines. She matted her photo on patterned papers and inked the edges.

supplies: Blue, white papers • Patterned papers (Chatterbox) • Metal frame (7 Gypsies) • Fiber (On the Surface) • Waxed floss • Metal charm (Marcella by Kay) • Alphabet beads • Safety pin • Computer font

Friends

Johanna Peterson, El Cajon, California

Stitching is a natural choice for adding feminine charm. Johanna chose colors to highlight the photo of her daughter's first trip to Build-a-Bear-Workshop and layered patterned papers for the background. Then, she stitched them to a piece of cardstock using various straight and zigzag patterns. She also stitched her photo directly to peach paper and adhered it to the page.

supplies: Peach, pink papers (Bazzill) • Patterned papers (Sonnets by Creative Imaginations, Current) • Flower dies (Quickutz) • Metal accents (All My Memories) • Tag • Foam stamps, rub-ons, paint, metal number, safety pin, jump ring, snaps (Making Memories) • Ribbon (Offray) • Rickrack (Wrights) • Flower charm (Hirschberg Schultz & Co.) • Computer font

The Sweetest Days

Courtney Walsh, Winnebago, Illinois

Simple cross-stitches add fashionable pop to this page. Courtney used the stitches to attach journaling strips, which she first inked and ran through buckles. After arranging her photos and accents on her paper, Courtney also added cross-stitches to the corners of the patterned paper. She also hand-stitched the letter buttons in place with embroidery floss.

supplies: Pink, blue papers (Die Cuts With a View) • Patterned paper (artist's own design) • Image-editing software • Ribbon slides, letter buttons (Junkitz) • Versacolor ink (Tsukineko) • Label maker (Dymo) • Embroidery floss • Black pen

All About Ted

Caroline Howe
Hornchurch, Essex, England

Machine-stitching serves three purposes on this page: It provides a subtle, flat accent, it helps define the large circular design elements and it secures everything to the page. Caroline finished the page by listing characteristics about her husband, Ted, with label tape.

supplies: Brown, tan, yellow, blue, green papers (Bazzill) • Foam stamps, paint (Making Memories) • Label maker (Dymo) • Embroidery floss

Swimming in a hotel pool is fun, but swimming with Granna and Poppa is SUPER special! On an overnight shopping trip to Memphis, Olivia and Michaela were very surprised to see their grandparents in the pool. They often swim with Granna in the summer, but having them both in the water was a first. Mommy was able to sit on the side and relax, while the grandparents did all the work.

Summer 2002

Swim Time

Angelia Wigginton
Belmont, Mississippi

Messy yet delicate strokes of paint add to this refreshing color scheme and accent the edges of the layered papers on Angelia's background. She placed her photos and then adhered painted chipboard letters on a strip on top of the background to create the title. The vertical title placement adds energy to the layout.

supplies: Blue, white papers (Bazzill) • Patterned papers (KI Memories, Autumn Leaves, Paper Fever, discontinued) • Rub-on, letter tiles (Doodlebug) • Chipboard letters, acrylic paint, button, circle tag (Making Memories) • Ribbon • Staples • Outdoors font (Autumn Leaves)

Moments

Kelli Lawlor, Norfolk, Virginia

Kelli rubbed an ink pad on all the edges of her papers and layered them to create this design. She crumpled both the tag and definition sticker, smoothed both of them flat and rubbed ink on the raised portions. The distressing and layers combined with the subtle colors result in a shabby-chic look and timeless feminine charm.

supplies: Green paper (Bazzill) • Patterned paper (Daisy D's) • Stickers (K & Co., Creative Imaginations, Li'l Davis, EK Success) • Jolee's Boutique key accent (EK Success) • Brads (Boxer) • Ribbon (Making Memories) • Waxy Flax (Scrapworks) • Stamping ink • Halda Normal font (fontpardise.com)

May 2004

Imagine

Valerie Maltais
Sherbrooke, Quebec, Canada

Valerie's use of black stamping ink to distress the elements of this page give it a timeless feel. The distressing is most noticeable on the journaling blocks—she rubbed the rounded edges with a black ink pad, concentrating color on the very edges for a distressed appearance. She also inked the silk flower to age it. The finishing touch comes on the photo, on which she created a framing effect with pink acrylic paint dry-brushed around the edges.

supplies: Patterned papers (Basicgrey) • Foam stamps, rub-ons (Making Memories) • Colorbox black stamping ink (Clearsnap) • Pink acrylic paint • Ribbon • Button • Silk flower • Computer fonts

My Love

Stephanie Rarick
Anchorage, Alaska

Stephanie rubbed embossed paper with an ink pad to enhance the raised design. The addition of black to the embossed paper helps to unify it with the other elements, while the red adds some color. She also inked the edges of her photo mat and applied chalk to the title.

supplies: Red paper (K & Co.) • Embossed paper (The Jennifer Collection, discontinued) • Script paper (Anna Griffin) • Tan paper, metal corners (Karen Foster) • Artistic Expressions transparency, Foofala letters, Afternoon Delight font (Autumn Leaves) • Twill letters (Carolee's Creations) • Stamping ink (Ranger) • Tag sticker (Pebbles) • Chalk (Stampin' Up) • Keyhole

The Caves

Katy Jurasevich, Valparaiso, Indiana

Using a block design keeps a layout clean and pure. Katy began with two tones of blue paper to highlight the cobalt blue skies in the photos. She accented with both a bright and an earthy green. The green frame and blue arrow work together to draw out a photo detail.

supplies: Blue, green papers (Bazzill) • Foam stamps, brads, definition sticker (Making Memories) • American Typewriter font (myfonts.com)

Ferkel Platz Pig Garden

Kim Mauch, Portland, Oregon

Using computer-editing software, Kim effectively cropped the photos to emphasize the important details of this collection of pigs. She created text boxes in which to house the title and journaling. Then she added digital accents in the form of ribbon and a photo turn.

supplies: Gina Cabrera digital papers, elements (digitaldesignessentials.com) • Image-editing software

Beach Finds

Heather Main
Langley, British Columbia, Canada

Heather created a uniform background using squares of patterned paper, omitting two squares to leave room for the title. She placed cropped pictures at an angle within the squares to add energy and movement. Heather double-matted the focal photo and layered it over two of the squares.

supplies: Blue, tan papers • Patterned paper (EK Success) • Letter rub-ons (Scrapworks) • Foam stamps, date stamps, word stamps (Making Memories) • Tim Holtz Distress Ink (Ranger) • Photo turns • Brads

Strawberry Field Forever

Jodi Heinen (Masters '05)

This page captures some of the toddler moments of Jodi's now much older daughter. Jodi created a wall of support photos to complement the engaging, enlarged focal photo. She stretched strips of paper and fabric across both sides of the layout to unify them. The title was inspired by the Beatles song, "Strawberry Fields Forever."

supplies: Blue, red papers • Fabric paper • Hannibal Lecter font (onescrappysite.com) • Litterbox ICG font (fonts.com) • Desyrel font (dafont.com)

Yoga Cat

Delany Butler, Fayetteville, Arkansas

Delany emphasized the horizontal nature of this cat's pose by printing the photo in a panoramic format so it would stretch across the layout. She used the rule of thirds to create this page. She horizontally divided her page in thirds for a balanced design that consists of three elements: the photo, the journaling and the title.

supplies: Patterned papers (Chatterbox, Basicgrey, Magenta, Karen Foster) • Alphabet stamps (PSX) • Letter sticker, page pebble (Making Memories) • Clip art • Jack Frost font (twopeasinabucket.com)

Spring Flowers

Erin Wells, Elsmere, Kentucky

Erin used circular shapes to both frame and mat photos on this layout about the renewal of life around her home with the arrival of spring. She accented paper rings with ribbon and stamped words. The curved shapes echo the organic shapes of the flowers and add contrast to the block shapes of the photos.

supplies: Green, purple papers (Bazzill) • Patterned paper (Chatterbox) • Letter stickers (American Crafts) • Rub-ons, ribbon (Making Memories) • Alphabet stamps (Hero Arts) • Stamping ink (Ranger) • Ribbon (Offray) • Fiber (EK Success) • Brads • Transparency • Computer font

Being at Hunting Island Beach brought back a lot of childhood memories for Al. This was the beach he would visit with his family. I know he enjoyed seeing his boys experience the beach like he did as a child.

I have never been a big fan of the water but spending time on this beach made me realize the peace that can be found there. It made me realize what large world is out there outside of our normal day-to-day environment. When there, it seems like nothing else in the world matters but the calmness found there. It made me wish we lived closer to the ocean.

This was Asa's second visit to the beach. This time he was a little older and could really understand what the ocean was all about. He had a fun time running with the waves and playing in the sand. What more could a boy ask for....lots of sand to dig in. He thought he was in heaven.

Brantly had such a fun time. Like always, he wasn't afraid of the water at all. He chased the waves til he could run no more. This environment fit his personality perfectly – he could play and run and NOT get into trouble. He took it all in and loved it, even though he didn't enjoy the taste of the water he took in too!

Baxter was a little stand-offish when it came to his view of the ocean – he was afraid of it. He didn't like how the sand would slide out from under his feet when the tide went out. He spent most of his time on the upper shore as an observer. After awhile, he got a little more daring and spent more time feeling the water.

Views of the Ocean

Wendy Tuten, Terrell, Texas

Wendy's journaling columns ebb and flow across her page just like waves wash to and from the shoreline. The different colors of the columns help move the eye across the page, and the thick bottom border of torn map patterned paper balances the overall design.

supplies: Brown, yellow, blue, green, red papers • Patterned paper (Rusty Pickle) • Paint, rub-ons (Making Memories) • Letters (Carolee's Creations) • Stamping ink (Ranger) • Ribbon • Bodoni font (myfonts.com)

My Greatest Love

Sue Thomas, Anoka, Minnesota

Sue created this mirror-image design with two enlarged photos that are each balanced with large elements—a tag and a flower, respectively. A bright green ribbon splits the page in two, and the words printed on it echo the title.

supplies: Brown, green papers (Bazzill) • Flower (Wal-Mart) • Foam stamp, brads (Making Memories) • Ribbon (May Arts) • Colorbox Fluid Chalk stamping ink (Clearsnap) • Versamark watermark ink (Tsukineko) • Zurich, Vladimir Script fonts (myfonts.com) • Wurth font (downloaded from the Internet)

Summer Sun

Kara Henry, Provo, Utah

For this page, Kara stamped paper strips to repeatedly echo the title. She then used them to frame her page. She embellished the frame with two sizes of brads, which adds a playful touch while also drawing attention to the frame. The monochromatic green color scheme is fresh and summery. Kara softened the harsh light on her son's face by converting her photos to black-and-white.

supplies: Green paper • Patterned paper (Doodlebug) • Alphabet stamps (Mobe) • Versacolor stamping ink (Tsukineko) • Rub-ons, spiral clip (Making Memories) • Eyelets (Creative Imaginations) • Fiber (Timeless Touches, Fiber Scraps) • Embroidery floss (DMC) • Brads • Computer font

13 Months

Alison Lockett, Knoxville, Tennessee

The bottom border looks as if the buttons attach the ribbon to the colorful circle patterns. But, they don't. To save time, Alison placed a strip of patterned paper across ribbons, which she had adhered to her background. Then she embellished the circle patterns with buttons. She cut the ribbon at angles for the polished look of tapered ends. The polka-dot patterns in the ribbon echo the polka dots found in the paper and the circle shape of the journaling block.

supplies: Yellow, pink papers (Bazzill) • Patterned paper, buttons, ribbon (SEI) • Stickers (American Crafts) • Rub-ons (Scrapworks) • Ribbon (Making Memories) • Century Gothic font (myfonts.com)

Lorynn

Michelle Coleman, Layton, Utah

The series of square accents bordering the bottom of this computer-generated page are little vignettes that display terms of endearment as well as the date. The same accents can be created by hand with squares of patterned paper, tags, a label maker, flower punch, brads and stickers.

supplies: Photoshop image-editing software (Adobe) • Diane Rigdon digital paper, accents (shabbyelements.com) • Computer fonts

Tremblant, QC

Gislaine Vincent
Dorval, Quebec, Canada

Filled with waterfalls and natural beauty, Gislaine spent her birthday traveling to Mont Tremblant with her husband. Gislaine created a photo border to capture the details with the help of preprinted tags that coordinate perfectly with her patterned paper. She cut her photos and mounted each half on separate tag shapes, lengthening the distance of the photo. Gislaine inked the edges of the tags and then layered them on her paper.

supplies: Patterned papers, tags, letter stickers, (Basicgrey) • Nick Bantock stamping ink (Ranger) • Computer fonts

Sweet or Sour

Angelia Wigginton, Belmont, Mississippi

With one child sweet and the other a bit sour, Angelia's daughters let her know what they thought of her impromptu photo shoot. For this slide-mount title, Angelia printed the words on vellum, cut them out and then matted them with yellow paper. She framed each word with slide mounts, which she further embellished with punched shapes and buttons. She connected the slide mounts with a piece of winding ribbon.

supplies: White paper (Bazzill) • Vellum • Patterned paper (KI Memories) • Buttons (Making Memories) • Slide mounts • Ribbon • Stand Tall font (twopeasinabucket.com)

Be the Artist

Stephanie Carpenter, Sandusky, Ohio

Even at a young age, Stephanie's son has enjoyed the process of being an artist. Stephanie wanted a cutting-edge look to capture this fact. She used foam stamps and acrylic paint to create her title on green paper. She individually cut each letter at angles, inked the edges and pieced them together on her page, creating a dynamic title with artistic flair and visual movement. She finished the title by accenting the bottom of each letter with staples.

supplies: Patterned paper, Rivets paper fasteners (Chatterbox) • Ribbon (Offray) • Colorbox Fluid Chalk stamping ink (Clearsnap) • Rub-on, foam stamps (Making Memories) • Staples • Paint • Computer font

Wish

Pam Sivage, Georgetown, Texas

Pam used various foam stamps and acrylic paint to create her title. The variety of sizes gives this page an antique-store aesthetic, which complements the subdued, classic patterns. She cut out each letter, layered it on a paper strip and stapled the definition of her title over the letters. She achieved the reflection of snow in her photo by taking it from the outside of her house through the storm door without using the flash.

supplies: Teal, cream papers (Prism) • Gin-X patterned papers, definition (Imagination Project) • Foam stamps, date stamp (Making Memories) • Foam stamps (Li'l Davis) • Paint (Delta) • Staples • Tab • Garamond font (linotype.com)

Gotcha

*Patti Milazzo for
Karen Foster Designs*

Patti created an attention-grabbing title with color and texture. First, she matted a vibrant, oversized letter sticker with blue and red papers. She then printed the remaining letters and cut them out individually. Patti finished by accenting the top of each letter with stapled ribbon.

supplies: Red, orange, blue papers, patterned papers, stickers, epoxy letter, metal plaque, Lacing brads, mini brads, Scrapper's Floss (Karen Foster) • Colorbox Fluid Chalk stamping ink (Clearsnap) • Yikes font (grsites.com)

Juggle

Kimberley Wood
Thousand Oaks, California

Using image-editing software, Kimberley created a frame that looks as if it is made from thin, stitched ribbon. Its angular and offset form help draw the eye to the photo and echo the movement of juggling. She framed her smaller photos with a similar ribbonlike design. Mimic this idea on a paper layout with pieces of ribbon or thin strips of paper. Secure the cross pieces with brads, eyelets or buttons.

supplies: Gina Carera digital ribbon (digitaldesignessentials.com) • Rhonna Farrar digital twill (scrapbook-bytes.com) • Angie Lanigan digital eyelets (scrapbook-bytes.com) • Image-editing software • Computer fonts

Bein' 3

Lisa Dorsey, Westfield, Indiana

Lisa recorded the nuances of her daughter at age 3 on this page. She printed some of her daughter's current phrases of choice on patterned paper and cut them into strips. She inked the edges of each section and pieced the sections around her photo to create a lively frame.

supplies: Green paper (Robin's Nest) • Patterned paper, letters (Carolee's Creation) • Ribbon, flower, page pebble (Making Memories) • Poem (Thena Smith) • Gilligan's Island font (downloaded from the Internet) • Broken 15 font (momscorner4kids.com)

Surfer Girl

Melissa Koehler
Surprise, Arizona

Melissa spent a weekend vacation with family, and she was able to see her sister-in-law get a surfboard for graduation. To highlight the event, she embellished a pink metal frame with ribbon and rub-on letters. Melissa placed the frame horizontally over her vertical photo, which she triple-matted. She layered various patterned papers horizontally and vertically on her page. These layers work with the matting and frame to create visual interest and emphasize the subject.

supplies: White paper (Bazzill) • Patterned paper, alphabet stamps (Rusty Pickle) • Foam stamps, chipboard letter, rub-ons, ribbon, metal frame (Making Memories) • Nick Bantock stamping ink (Ranger) • Bert font (dafont.com)

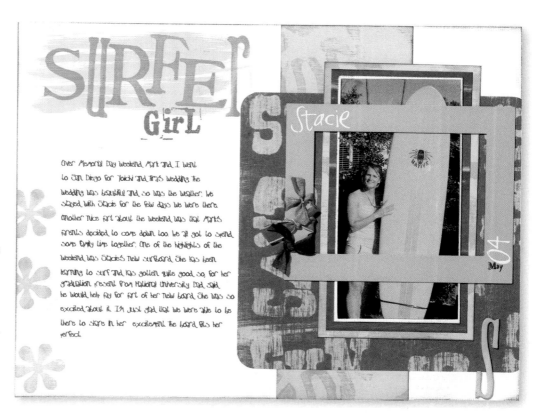

Happy Moments

Maggie Holmes for Making Memories

Maggie recorded the happy moments of her son's third birthday party on this page. To really capture her son's gleeful expression, she placed a metal frame around his face and wrapped one side of it with various ribbons, securing them with brads and knots. For the background, Maggie layered various papers together and stitched them at the seams.

supplies: Blue, orange papers, patterned papers, metal frame, snaps, brads, photo anchors, stitched tin tile, rub-on letters, ribbon, chipboard letters (Making Memories)

product guide

The following companies manufacture the products featured in this book.
Check your local scrapbook retailer or arts-and-crafts store to find the products.

3M Stationery
800-364-3577 3m.com

7 Gypsies
877-7GYPSY7 7gypsies.com

Adobe™
adobe.com

All My Memories
888-553-1998 allmymemories.com

American Crafts
800-879-5185 americancrafts.com
(wholesale only)

Anna Griffin, Inc.
888-817-8170 annagriffin.com
(wholesale only)

Arctic Frog
arcticfrog.net

Autumn Leaves
800-588-6707

BasicGrey
basicgrey.com

Bazzill Basics Paper
480-558-8557 bazzillbasics.com

Blumenthal Lansing Co.
563-538-4211 buttonsplus.com

Bo-Bunny Press
801-771-4010 bobunny.com

Boxer Scrapbook Productions
503-625-0455
boxerscrapbooks.com

C. R. Gibson
800-243-6004 crgibson.com

C & T Publishing
ctpub.com

Cardeaux Trimmings
cardeauxtrimmings.com

CARL Mfg. USA, Inc.
800-257-4771 carl-products.com
(wholesale only)

Carolee's Creations®
435-563-1100 ccpaper.com

Chatterbox, Inc.
208-939-9133 chatterboxinc.com

Clearsnap®, Inc.
800-448-4862 clearsnap.com
(wholesale only)

Close To My Heart
888-655-6552 closetomyheart.com

Club Scrap™, Inc.
888-634-9100 clubscrap.com

Colorbök™, Inc.
800-366-4660 colorbok.com
(wholesale only)

Craf-T Products
507-236-3996 craftproducts.com

Crafter's Workshop, The
877-CRAFTER
thecraftersworkshop.com

Creative Imaginations
800-942-6487 cigift.com
(wholesale only)

Creative Impressions
719-596-4860
creativeimpressions.com

Creek Bank Creations
creekbankcreations.com

Croppin' Companion, The
croppincompanion.com

Cross-My-Heart
888-689-8808
crossmyheart.com

C-Thru® Ruler Company, The
800-243-8419 cthruruler.com
(wholesale only)

Current®, Inc.
800-848-2848
TimesToCherish.com

Daisy D's Paper Company
888-601-8955 daisydspaper.com

Darice, Inc.
800-321-1494 darice.com

Delta Technical Coatings, Inc.
800-423-4135 deltacrafts.com

Design Originals
800-877-7820
d-originals.com

Designer's Library, The
designerslibrary.com

Destination Scrapbook Designs
866-806-7826
destinationstickers.com

Die Cuts With a View™
801-224-6766
diecutswithaview.com

DMC Corporation
973-589-0606
dmc-usa.com

DMD Industries, Inc.
800-805-9890 dmdind.com
(wholesale only)

Doodlebug Design™
801-952-0555 doodlebug.ws

Dymo
dymo.com

EK Success™, Ltd.
800-524-1349 eksuccess.com
(wholesale only)

Eyelet Outlet
eyeletoutlet.com

Fancy Pants Designs, LLC
fancypantsdesigns.com

Fiber Scraps
215-230-4905 fiberscraps.com

Frances Meyer®, Inc.
800-372-6237 francesmeyer.com

Fredrix
fredrixprintcanvas.com

Heart & Home
888-616-6166 melissafrances.com

Heidi Grace Designs
253-973-5542 heidigrace.com

Hero Arts® Rubber Stamps, Inc.
800-822-4376 heroarts.com
(wholesale only)

Hirschberg Schultz & Co.
800-221-8640
(wholesale only)

Hot Off The Press, Inc.
800-227-9595 craftpizazz.com

Hunt Corp.
hunt-corp.com

Imagination Project, Inc.
imaginationproject.com

Jennifer Collection, The
thejennifercollection.com

Jesse James and Company
610-435-0201
jessejamesbutton.com

Jo-Ann Fabrics
joannfabrics.com

Junkitz
junkitz.com

K & Company
888-244-2083 kandcompany.com

Karen Foster Design™
801-451-9779
karenfosterdesign.com
(wholesale only)

KI Memories
972-243-5595 kimemories.com

Kopp Design
801-489-6011 koppdesign.com

Krylon
800-4KRYLON

La Pluma, Inc.
debrabeagle.com

Lasting Impressions for Paper, Inc.
800-9-EMBOSS

Leave Memories
leavememories.com

Leisure Arts
800-643-8030
leisurearts.com

Li'l Davis Designs
949-838-0344
lildavisdesigns.com

Ma Vinci's Reliquary
crafts.dm.net/mall/reliquary

Magenta Rubber Stamps
800-565-5254
magentastyle.com
(wholesale only)

Magic Scraps™
972-238-1838
magicscraps.com

Making Memories
800-286-5263
makingmemories.com

Marcella by Kay
exclusively for Target
target.com

Marvy® Uchida
800-541-5877 uchida.com
(wholesale only)

May Arts
mayarts.com (wholesale only)

Me & My Big Ideas
949-583-2065
meandmybigideas.com
(wholesale only)

Memories Complete
866-966-6365
memoriescomplete.com

Memory Stitches
317-410-7387
memorystitches.com

Michaels® Arts & Crafts
800-642-4235 michaels.com

MoBe Stamps
mobestamps.com

Mostly Animals
800-832-8886
mostlyanimals.com

Mrs. Grossman's
mrsgrossmans.com

My Mind's Eye, Inc.
801-298-3709
frame-ups.com

National Cardstock
866-452-7120

Offray & Son, Inc.
offray.com

On the Surface
847-675-2520

Paper House Productions
paperhouseproductions.com

Paper Loft, The
801-254-1961 paperloft.com
(wholesale only)

Paperfever
800-477-0902 paperfever.com

Pebbles, Inc.
pebblesinc.com

Plaid Enterprises, Inc.
800-842-4197 plaidonline.com

Prima Marketing, Inc.
primamarketinginc.com

Prism
prismpapers.com

Provo Craft®
888-577-3545 provocraft.com
(wholesale only)

PSX Design™
800-782-6748 psxdesign.com

Purple Onion Designs
purpleoniondesigns.com

QuickKutz®
888-702-1146 quickutz.com

Ranger Industries, Inc.
800-244-2211 rangerink.com

Reminisce
319-358-9777
designsbyreminisce.com

Royal & Langnickel
royalbrush.com

Rubba Dub Dub Artist's Stamps
707-748-0929 artsanctum.com/
RubbaDubDubHome.html

Rusty Pickle
801-746-1045 rustypickle.com

Sanook
800-445-5565
sanookpaper.com

Scenic Route Paper Co.
scenicroutepaper.com

Scrapworks, LLC
scrapworks.com

SEI, Inc.
800-333-3279 shopsei.com

Stampin' Up!®
800-782-6787 stampinup.com

Therm O Web, Inc.
800-323-0799 thermoweb.com
(wholesale only)

Timeless Touches
623-362-8285
timelesstouches.net

Tsukineko®, Inc.
800-769-6633 tsukineko.com

Wal-Mart
walmart.com

Waste Not Paper
800-867-2737
wastenotpaper.com

Weathered Door, The
theweathereddoor.com

Westrim/Memories Forever
800-727-2727 westrimcrafts.com

Wordsworth Stamps
719-282-3495
wordsworthstamps.com

Wrights® Ribbon Accents
877-597-4448

We have made every attempt to properly credit the items mentioned in this book. If any company has
been listed incorrectly, please contact Darlene D'Agostino at darlene.dagostino@fwpubs.com.